New Studies in the Philosophy of Rel...

General Editor: W. D. Hudson
University of Exeter

This series of monographs includes studies of all the main problems in the philosophy of religion. It will be of particular interest to those who study this subject in universities or colleges. The philosophical problems connected with religious belief are not, however, a subject of concern only to specialists; they arise in one form or another for all intelligent men when confronted by the appeals or the claims of religion.

The general approach of this series is from the standpoint of contemporary analytical philosophy, and the monographs are written by a distinguished team of philosophers, all of whom now teach, or have recently taught, in British or American universities. Each author has been commissioned to analyse some aspect of religious belief; to set forth clearly and concisely the philosophical problems which arise from it; to take into account the solutions which classical or contemporary philosophers have offered; and to present his own critical assessment of how religious belief now stands in the light of these problems and their proposed solutions.

In the main it is theism with which these monographs deal, because that is the type of religious belief with which readers are most likely to be familiar, but other forms of religion are not ignored. Some of the authors are religious believers and some are not, but it is not their primary aim to write polemically, much less dogmatically, for or against religion. Rather, they set themselves to clarify the nature of religious belief in the light of modern philosophy by bringing into focus the questions about it which a reasonable man as such has to ask. How is talk of God like, and how unlike, other universes of discourse in which men engage, such as science, art or morality? Is this talk of God self-consistent? Does it accord with other rational beliefs which we hold about man or the world which he inhabits? It is questions such as these which this series will help the reader to answer for himself.

New Studies in the Philosophy of Religion

IN THE SAME SERIES

Morality and Religion

WILLIAM WARREN BARTLEY III
Professor of Philosophy, University of Pittsburgh

Macmillan
St Martin's Press

First published 1971 by
MACMILLAN AND CO LTD
London and Basingstoke
Associated companies in New York Toronto
Dublin Melbourne Johannesburg and Madras

Library of Congress catalog card no. 71-124948

SBN 333 10277 0

Printed in Great Britain by
ROBERT MACLEHOSE AND CO LTD
The University Press, Glasgow

One paradox, however, must be accepted and this is that it is necessary to continually attempt the seemingly impossible.

Hermann Hesse
The Journey to the East (p. 7)

For Stephen Kresge

Contents

Editor's Preface

The logical relationship between morality and religion has been a matter of controversy amongst philosophers and theologians from the earliest times and it continues to be a subject of lively debate. The 'is–ought problem', as it is called, becomes particularly acute in the present connexion. How are religious beliefs about what God's will *is* logically related to moral judgements as to what men *ought* to do? Is there a logical gap between the *is* and the *ought* here? Or is the *ought* groundless apart from the *is*? Some thinkers hold to the former view, some to the latter. This monograph's main purpose is to clear up the points at issue and to find some solution to the problem.

Like other contributions to the series *New Studies in the Philosophy of Religion*, it combines exposition with criticism. Professor Bartley reviews the discussion of the relationship between religion and morality from Plato's question 'Do the gods love piety because it is pious, or is it pious because they love it?' to the ideas of modern intellectuals such as Keynes and Woolf concerning the proper connexion between religion, in the sense of 'one's attitude towards oneself and the ultimate', and morality in the sense of 'one's attitude towards the outside world and the intermediate'. Amongst many other subjects, the author deals with the attempt by some philosophers to reduce religion to morality reinforced by stories and the attempt of theologians such as Kierkegaard or Barth to show that morality is not derivable from religion or vice versa. Throughout he combines clear explanations of what distinguished thinkers have said with highly original criticisms and suggestions of his own. His very individual treatment of the 'is – ought question' and his discussion of whether in the light of the most profound psychological insights available to us it makes any sense to say that men ought to act morally are but two of the many subjects on which his opinions are calculated to arouse lively interest and controversy.

This study, short though it is, will therefore not only be invaluable to the student who is reading philosophy or philosophy of religion at college or university, but it will be received with interest by professional philosophers and theologians as a scholarly and penetrating contribution to thought about both religion and morality.

W. D. Hudson

University of Exeter

Preface

The larger part of the material contained in this study is drawn from the research and writing I did during my tenure of the S. A. Cook Bye-Fellowship in Philosophy of Religion at Gonville and Caius College, Cambridge University. So it is an especial pleasure to take this opportunity to express my gratitude to the Master and Fellows of Gonville and Caius College for their hospitality and for the growth in my intellectual, moral and religious experience which it afforded.

W. W. Bartley III

Schenley Heights
Pittsburgh
Christmas 1969

1 The Reduction of Morality to Religion

The chief aim of this study is to get clearer about the extent to which morality and religion may be interdependent. I propose to begin by assuming, as others have done, that there is some such thing as morality and some such thing as religion, and I shall take as my first task the clarification of what would be involved in the interdependence of these two things. We shall avoid danger of serious muddle only if we bear firmly in mind that our initial investigation of dependence relationships is preliminary, and that we must also ask what sorts of things that might be called morality and religion could be dependent or independent in the ways charted.

I

Two logical relationships possibly relevant to the question of the dependence of one thing on another are derivability and compatibility. With regard to the logical relationships obtaining between their statements, morality and religion are either derivable one from the other or not, and they are either compatible or not.

Six important alternatives can be charted in terms of these relationships. First, morality may be derivable from religion *and* vice versa. In this case morality and religion are identical. Second, morality may be derivable from religion but not vice versa. Morality is a part but not the whole of religion. Third, religion may be derivable from morality but not vice versa. Religion is a part but not the whole of morality. In these first three cases, morality and religion must be compatible; no conflict between them could exist. The fourth case is that in which morality is not derivable from religion or vice versa *but* in which they are fully compatible one with the other. Here the two are not identical, nor is one a part of the other, but they are consistent – and independent. In the fifth case, morality is not derivable from religion or vice versa and the two are incompatible to at least some extent but not wholly: some of the statements of the one are compatible with some of the statements of the other, and some not. Finally, in the sixth case, morality and religion are totally incompatible. They are mutually exclusive.

I know of no one who has maintained the sixth alternative. But each of the first five has been maintained at one time or other by some philosopher or theologian.

II

On first reading, Theodore Parker's essay on 'The Transient and the Permanent in Christianity' appears to provide an example of the first position. 'Christianity', he writes, 'is a simple thing, very simple. It is absolute, pure morality.'[1] While Parker may appear to be identifying morality and religion, closer reading of this essay together with his other work suggests that what he wants to express is his conviction that morality is the *essential*, the permanent and unchanging thing about religion, not the whole of it. Similar things can be said of most other writers who appear to be identifying morality and religion. Whilst one may say 'Morality *is* religion', and another 'Religion *is* morality', they rarely intend any identification of the two. This is one of two reasons for passing quickly over the first position and beginning with the second: namely, that morality is derivable from religion. A more important reason is that, were morality and religion really identical, the problems of this study would hardly arise. And in any case, the second position is the one in which philosophers have, for better or for worse, shown most interest.

Some theologians and religious writers have found the second position particularly attractive, just as critics of religion have found it important to defeat. The appeal to the religious believer of the idea that morality may be derivable from religion is hardly difficult to explain. For while religion is under heavy criticism from contemporary thinkers, few of them have been so bold as to cast aspersions on morality. So if it could be shown that morality was logically derivable

2

from religion, this would provide added support for the semi-sociological convictions of some religious believers that society would give way to 'moral anarchy' were acceptance of religion to wane.

An ancient philosophical argument can, however, be used to show that morality is *not* dependent on religion. This argument, parts of which are found in Plato's *Euthyphro*, is now usually argued in terms of the question: 'Is *x* good because God wills it or does God will *x* because it is good?' This question is usually presented as one about the logical relationships obtaining amongst various kinds of statements, and embedded in an argument which takes the following course. Whether God does or does not will certain things is a matter of fact – perhaps not ascertainable fact, but fact all the same. Statements about what is good are statements not of fact but of value. These positions I share. At this point in the argument some reference to the mistake of deriving 'ought' (value) statements from 'is' (factual) statements is introduced. It is pointed out that statements about value cannot be derived from statements about fact; and *it then may be concluded that there can therefore be no logical relationship between statements of fact and statements of value. This conclusion I reject*, and with it I reject further conclusions based upon it that there can be no relationship of a logical character between statements concerning morality and religious statements of a factual character.

To develop this argument and support the claims just made – and to evaluate the traditional 'Euthyphro argument' concerning morality and religion, one has to consider just what is involved in deriving one statement from another logically – in this case statements about value from statements about fact. To this task the remainder of this chapter is devoted.

III

It is an elementary but central point of logic that a valid derivation is one in which when the premises are true the conclusion must also be true. If any given conclusion can be validly derived from a particular premise then it is equal to or else logically weaker than the premise: and by the same token, in such an argument the premises are equal to or logically stronger than the conclusion. In no circumstances may a stronger statement be validly derived from a weaker one.

In the following, I shall be primarily concerned with statements that are stronger or weaker than one another in this sense. But since I have mentioned that statements equal in strength may be derived one from the other, it may be useful to take as our first example of a valid argument such a case. Thus:

Premise:	Soames Forsyte had no foresight
Conclusion:	Soames Forsyte had no foresight

is a valid derivation. Here the premise and conclusion, being identical, are equal in strength. And it is obviously impossible for this derivation to be invalid. Here is a clear case in which it would be impossible for the premise to be true without the conclusion being true as well.

Consider another example of a valid argument:

Premise:	Soames Forsyte had much foresight, (and) Soames Forsyte had little feeling
Conclusion:	Soames Forsyte had much foresight.

Here is an example of a valid argument in which the premise is not equal to but stronger than the conclusion, richer in content than the conclusion. And here again, the argument is valid precisely because when the premise is true then the conclusion *must* be true.

To produce an instance of an invalid argument, we may easily juggle our example. Thus the argument:

Premise:	Soames Forsyte had little feeling
Conclusion:	Soames Forsyte had much foresight but little feeling.

is invalid. The conclusion is stronger than is the premise. Although both premise and conclusion here *may* be true, that

4

is a contingent matter having nothing to do with the validity of the argument: the conclusion here *need not* be true when the premise is true. Possibly Soames Fosyte is poorly endowed with both foresight and feeling – a possibility not excluded by this argument.

I have dwelt on these very elementary logical points – ones which might on the face of it seem irrelevant to our inquiry – precisely because they are so familiar and elementary that their importance in a particular situation may easily be overlooked. Indeed, some of the central problems of philosophy are little more than illustrations of different sorts of situations in which a conclusion cannot be derived logically from a premise that is weaker than it.

To come to the point: there is no denying that the 'Is/Ought' Question and the Problem of Induction are two central problems of philosophy. And the well-known mistake of deriving evaluative (ought) conclusions from descriptive (is) premises has in common with Inductive Reasoning at least this much: both arise from attempts to derive stronger conclusions from weaker premises.

Take a straightforward example of inductive argument:

Premise: Soames is a Forsyte and is rich
             James is a Forsyte and is rich
             Jolyon is a Forsyte and is rich
             _____

Conclusion: All Forsytes are rich.

This simple textbook illustration of inductive reasoning is of course invalid. There may well be some Forsyte who is not rich. Only if Soames, James and Jolyon were the only Forsytes could the inference be valid – and even then only if this additional information were added to the premise, thus strengthening it. A better illustration of inductive reasoning, more satisfactory to the symbolic logician or philosopher of science, would take as one's conclusion an 'All' statement covering an infinite number of cases – as our example does not, since the number of Forsytes is presumably finite however great their wealth. But the example suffices to make the point.

Now consider the sort of argument that one might and indeed can find in moral argument:

Premise:	x is conducive to the greatest happiness of the greatest number, and x is good.
	y is conducive to the greatest happiness of the greatest number, and y is good.
	z is conducive to the greatest happiness of the greatest number, and z is good.
Conclusion:	All things which are conducive to the greatest happiness of the greatest number are good.

Here embodied in one example we find a conclusion about what is good *and* a straightforward example of inductive reasoning. The argument happens to be invalid. But what is curious is that persons who discuss such arguments sometimes say that the reason that they are invalid is that a conclusion about goodness or value has been derived from statements about matters of fact or past experience. But this information – even if it were correct, as it is not (the premises are by no means purely descriptive!) – has *nothing* to do with the reason why the argument is invalid. The argument is invalid because it is inductive; and an inductive argument is invalid because its conclusion is stronger than the collective strength of its premises.

Another element, not yet mentioned, is involved in both the Is/Ought mistake and in inductive reasoning. In both cases we have statements the merits of which must be decided – in the first instance these statements being of an evaluative character and in the second instance the statements being scientific projections about the future or 'universal statements'. The problem is to 'justify' these statements, taken as the conclusions of arguments of justification, when it can be shown that the available justifiers, or statements which might be used as premises in such a justifying argument, are not sufficiently strong to entail the statements in question. A scientific statement of universal form cannot be derived from, justified by, a finite set of observation statements considered evidence for it. Nor can a statement about goodness, or about what one ought to do, be derived from, justified by, factual information alone. Moreover, even when – as in our example – evaluative material is added to what is descriptive in the premises, that alone does not suffice to entail the evaluative conclusion. The premise must be *strong enough* to entail the conclusion. To some of these problems we shall return later. First we need to relate the discussion of this section to the question of the relationship of morality and religion.

IV

An important reason for this preliminary excursion into the Is/Ought question and inductive reasoning, and into the question of the logical relations that may obtain amongst various kinds of statements has been to provide a better purchase on what I have called the 'Euthyphro Argument' concerning morality and religion.

A minor historical licence has been taken in dubbing this argument the 'Euthyphro Argument', since although a similar argument is to be found in Plato's *Euthyphro*, the formulation as well as the structure of the argument is somewhat different. Plato discusses the question: 'Do the gods love piety (ὅσιον) because it is pious, or is it pious because they love it?'[2] To avoid any problem of historical or philological exegesis connected with Greek concepts of piety or divinity, I have taken the liberty, as have those other modern and contemporary writers who have traced this question to the *Euthyphro*, of rephrasing the question as: 'Is *x* good because God wills it or does God will *x* because it is good?'

If one answers this question by affirming that *x* is good because God wills it, one commits – or at least appears to commit – the Is/Ought mistake. One derives or justifies the goodness of *x* from what is taken to be the fact that God wills *x*. One is deriving an evaluative statement from a factual statement. On the other hand, if one says that God wills *x* because it is good, it appears that the goodness of *x* is independent of God's wishes, or to put the matter differently, that morality is radically independent of the wishes of God.

One's answer to this question bears importantly on one's assessment of the nature of the interdependence of morality and religion, but it does not, as some persons have supposed, bear on the question whether one is religious, let alone on the question whether one is a Christian. For instance, although both St Thomas Aquinas and William of Occam were Christian theologians, Thomas concluded that God willed something

7

because it was good, whereas William thought God's commandment the very basis of goodness.

The Euthyphro question can now be clarified schematically in terms of our discussion in the previous section. Take the following inference:

Premise: God wills x
_____
Conclusion: x is good.

Taken out of context these two statements appear to be independent and the inference invalid: one cannot derive q from p, or vice versa. Our conclusion here no more follows from the premise than the premise follows from the conclusion. So the inference is invalid *quite regardless* of the evaluative character of the conclusion and the presumably factual character of the premise.

It is, of course possible to make our conclusion follow from an *augmented* premise which not only includes the original premise but also appears prima facie to provide a reasonable context for the argument. For instance:

Premise: God wills x
                If God wills x then x is good
_____
Conclusion: x is good..

This argument is formally valid; but possibly an exorbitant price has been paid for validity, and without any dependence of morality on religion even having been shown. A great deal will depend on the way we interpret the added premise: 'If God wills x then x is good.' It might be interpreted as a 'meaning rule'. Someone might say that what is *meant* by 'good' is 'something conforming to God's will'. But such a move is highly unsatisfactory. For one thing, it turns the added premise into a triviality. For now 'If God wills x then x is good' means, by substitution, 'If God wills x then x is something conforming to God's will.' In short, 'God wills what God wills.' Moreover, were such an interpretation taken, then the inference from 'God wills x' to 'x is good' would be a tautological transformation.

8

Nor is it any help to say that 'something conforming to God's will' is not *the* meaning of 'good' but how 'we' or some class of persons mean or use 'good'. Non-Christians do indeed use the word 'good' differently. But even within the so-called Judeo-Christian tradition there has been debate about whether what God wills is good – consider the Book of Job. Thus it seems pointless to say that even Christians *mean* by 'good' 'something conforming to God's will', let alone that this is *the* meaning of 'good'. The question we are dealing with is not a verbal one; or rather, if it *is* a verbal question, it is perhaps not worth dealing with.

Another interpretation of the statement 'If God wills x then x is good' is that it is a synthetic *causal* statement. In effect, what is meant is that if God wills x, then that renders x good. It is important to notice, as regards this interpretation, that *if* it is correct, then the question whether morality is derivable from religion is not settled. On the one hand, an evaluative statement: 'x is good', *has* been derived from premises pertaining to religion. On the other hand, two premises were required: (1) God wills x, and (2) If God wills x then x is good. But the second premise is also evaluative, and so the question whether morality is derivable from religion is simply shifted back a step. If we disallow such a shift, then difficulties in the interpretation of 'If God wills x then x is good' as a synthetic statement persist. First, this interpretation simply *begs the question* whether morality is dependent on religion. It appears that we have to choose between shifting the question and begging the question. To avoid begging the question we would have to advance some reason to justify our claim that God's willing of x renders x good. How would this be done? How do we know that when God wills x, then x is good? To suggest that this is something known on faith is unsatisfactory since faith may be defined as a deliberate self-conscious begging of the question. Another possible answer is to say that we know this from experience. The difficulty here is that this answer appears to commit us to the Is/Ought mistake – viz., we appear to be claiming that we *can* justify an evaluative statement by appealing to experience. But even if we overlook this, difficulties still remain. Suppose we were to argue that by appealing to experience we mean to claim that in all past cases experienced by us, whenever God has willed something, that something has turned out to be good.

9

Several questions jump at one when one considers such a claim. Do we ever in fact have experience of God's willing something? There is no straightforward answer, unless what is meant by 'experience' is, say, the expressions or demonstrations of God's will that are reported in certain putative sources of revelation, such as the Bible.

What about the other part of the claim? *Do* we ever experience something's turning out to be good, or something's being good? Since there is some sense, however unclear, in which we do experience things as good, it is presumably legitimate to answer this question affirmatively.

But one thing we do not experience is a causal relationship between God's willing something and the goodness of that thing. Even were we to assume that we do have experience of God's willing something, and even if we do have experience in some as yet unclear sense of things being good, we have no experience of a causal relationship obtaining between these two. At best – on the assumption that we are privy to God's will – we have an experience of constant conjunction between those things willed by God and those things we experience as good. In this case, two problems arise.

First, it would appear that we can experience something as good independently of experiencing it as willed by God; a constant conjunction, even if it existed, would provide no evidence for the *causal* claim that x is good because God wills it.

Secondly, as we might expect from this rather Humean argument, we are involved in inductive reasoning and invalid inference. Frame the situation schematically:

Premise:	God willed a and a was good
	God willed b and b was good
	God willed c and c was good
	God willed d and d was good
Conclusion:	Whatever God wills is good.

Like all inductive arguments, this argument is invalid. But even if it were – *per impossibile* – valid, it would still not justify the claim that x is good because God wills it. Which brings us

10

back to the problem of causation: even if whatever God wills is as a matter of fact good, we might say that he wills it *because it is good*. It is not necessary to deny that whatever God wills is good in order to deny that something is good because God wills it. Indeed, the only way to prevent a denial that something is good because God wills it is to claim that something becomes good only by God's willing it *and is otherwise not good*.

This conclusion, however, puts us in a rather curious position. We have just reviewed a number of difficulties that arise when one attempts to derive the claim that something is good from the information that God wills it by means of adding the further premise, 'Whatever God wills is good.' Now it appears that even if we *could* satisfactorily defend the claim that whatever God wills is good, we still would not have addressed ourselves in an acceptable way to the Euthyphro question. Our problem comes to this: *derivability, even were it possible, is not enough*. We are concerned with the causal dependence of morality on religion, a relationship that cannot be captured by the mere derivability – even if that were possible – of moral statements from religious statements. In order to establish that something is good because God wills it *and not vice versa*, we must show that morality is *solely* dependent on religion, or derivable solely from religious statements. This we have not done: effects can be produced by a plurality of *different* causes; conclusions can be derived validly from a plurality of different premises. Possibly many things – God's will amongst them – could render things and actions good. God's will would be *sufficient* to render something good without being *necessary* to render something good. To probe the difficulties here is to open a Pandora's Box for philosophical analysis. For example, when we begin to examine the possible combinations of necessary and sufficient conditions, we find that quite intricate accounts of the dependence and independence of morality and religion are possible. There is for example the following difficulty. Where many moral decisions are concerned, no directive of a religious character is available. So that, even if one were to accept that one ought to do what God wills, one would still have to ascertain by moral reasoning independent of religious teaching what to do in those situations concerning which God had not spoken to us. In line with such difficulties is an interesting essay by Professor Peter Geach, who suggests that a knowledge of God is *not* prerequisite to our

11

having *any* moral knowledge. A knowledge of God's will is not *always* necessary. But it is, according to Geach, sometimes necessary and always sufficient.[3]

In sum: in order to derive the statement '*x* is good' from the premise 'God wills *x*', we should have to augment that premise with a further premise that turns out to be highly problemmatic. And even if we could – *per impossibile* – overcome these problems, we should still not have charted a dependence relationship between morality and religion that would satisfy many theologians: we would not have satisfied the theologian who maintains that morality is solely dependent on religion, nor would we have satisfied the more modest theologian, like Geach, who maintains only that morality is *sometimes* dependent on God's will.

V

Before turning to the next part of our argument, it may be wise to repeat a point that hopefully is already clear. *That what God wills is good has not been denied in the foregoing*. What has been suggested is that there appears to be no reason to support the claim that something is good only if or because God wills it, let alone the weaker claim that would suffice to insure derivability of '*x* is good' from 'God wills *x*'. So we have challenged the first alternative in the Euthyphro question: that *x* is good because God wills it; and we have said nothing as yet in criticism of the second alternative: namely, that God wills *x* because *x* is good.

Indeed, if a certain *x* were good, then that would help *explain* why God, purportedly an all-benevolent being, would will it. For the reasons given we cannot explain the goodness of something by the fact (if it is a fact) that God wills it; but the contrary might be possible. A comparable confusion is sometimes made by philosophers in regard to our intuitions of what is correct. For instance, the fact that something appears intuitively convincing or self-evidently true is not sufficient to guarantee its truth. However, *if* it is true then that may *explain* why it appears intuitively convincing or self-evidently true to us. The confusions here are not identical, but they are similar in character.

12

The foregoing discussion would appear to support the view that evaluative statements cannot be justified by, i.e., derived from, factual statements, any more than scientific theories can be justified by, i.e., derived from, observation statements. The possible novelty of the presentation has been to indicate that the reasons for this – having to do with logical strength – are identical in both cases.

From what has been said, however, it is not possible to draw a conclusion which is all too often drawn in such discussions: namely, that no logical relationship is possible between observational statements and scientific theories on the one hand, or between evaluative statements and factual statements on the other hand.

That observational statements may bear logically on theoretical scientific statements is a point that has been made frequently in recent years.[4] For an asymmetry exists between justificatory argument and critical argument which permits just such logical relations. Thus if we take a controversial scientific theory not as the conclusion of a justifying argument but rather as a *premise* in a critical argument, we find that an observational statement may be related to it through *modus tollens*. The falsification of an observational statement made on the basis of the scientific theory in question leads to the falsification of the premise in which that scientific theory occurred.

That a comparable situation obtains in moral argumentation has not been noticed. I propose to show that a moral statement can sometimes be logically falsified by a factual statement in a *modus tollens* argument, and that logical relations thus obtain between factual and evaluative or normative statements in at least some cases. That the argument about to follow bears on religion can be seen in that the example of a moral statement used is rather like a 'Counsel of Perfection' – of which the perfect example is, of course: 'Be ye therefore perfect, even as your Father which is in heaven is perfect.'

The following argument will assume as correct the doctrine that 'ought' statements imply 'can' statements *in respect to persons*. Thus, in saying that a person ought to do something, we assume that it is *possible* for him to do that thing, that he *can* do that thing. I have italicised the phrase 'in respect to *persons*'

13

because I do not wish to claim that it is always true that 'ought' statements imply 'can' statements. For example, I see no point to objecting to the statement that, say, 'the world ought to be different', by saying that the world cannot be different – even if we could show that the latter were so. It seems perfectly sensible, without logical contradiction, to maintain at one and the same time that the world ought to be different *and* that it cannot be different. But this interesting issue is not one that need concern us here; which is a further reason for my restricting my remarks to 'ought' and 'can' statements about persons. So when I write ' "ought" implies "can" ', I should be understood as referring only to cases where persons are concerned.

On our assumption, the following argument is valid:

Premise: Jones ought to be a genius

Conclusion: Jones can be a genius.

And suppose that we have evidence indicating that the conclusion is false. We might learn, for instance, that Jones is suffering from extensive organic brain damage, or that he has an 'I.Q.' unusually below normal. Whilst one might reasonably question the results of an I.Q. test, one probably would accept sound evidence of massive brain damage as proof that it is false that Jones can be a genius. But then, by *modus tollens*, it is false that Jones ought to be a genius. And we have used a factual consideration in evaluation and criticism of a moral statement.

Take a more topical example, the punishment of criminals, an issue both of morality and of public policy – and a controversial question amongst religious thinkers. Suppose that one argues that one ought not to punish criminals but to treat them all psychologically in order to cure them of criminal tendencies. To this proposal it may be retorted that 'ought' implies 'can', and that there exist some criminals – for example, those with certain genetic defects – whom it is impossible to cure by psychological treatment. The example is not fanciful: the XYY chromosomal abnormality has been widely associated by researchers with criminal behaviour and/or low intelligence in adult males; and recent studies suggest that one male in 300

14

may be born with just this abnormality.[5] This factual information, which bears logically on the original proposal for a different public policy, will if taken seriously lead to a modification of the proposal. Dr Park S. Gerald, of the Harvard Medical School, has urged that a large-scale study of XYY incidence should be done, because a 'great deal of social planning could be related to this. These people [with XYY syndrome] might still get into trouble despite present welfare programs.'[6] Since such arguments can easily be misused, perhaps it is necessary for me to add here that a demonstration that one proposed alternative to punishment runs into difficulties in certain cases is in itself no argument on behalf of punishment. Whatever the facts concerning the XYY chromosomal abnormality may be, the problem of punishment remains to be dealt with.

Such arguments in which ' "ought" implies "can" '. can be used to enable factual claims to rebut prescriptive remarks are by no means unusual. Quite the contrary, they are rather common. Bishop Robinson provided an interesting illustration when he reported the response to his proposal that capital punishment be abolished in favour of attempts to reform even the most hardened criminals. The response is reported in the *Observer* as follows:

Then came the letters; a week after the sermon they were piled on chairs and the floor in his study, a tide of sour disagreement. . . . 'Well, you bloody fool,' one began. A woman from Hampstead wrote briefly to say that 'There *are* evil men who are unredeemable.' 'This is all rot,' claimed an anonymous writer. 'Just HANG 'em. I say dam the church and such talk.'[7] :

In the *Observer* article from which these excerpts are taken, no mention of the XYY chromosomal abnormality is made. And outside an informed medical context the claim that there just *are* 'unredeemable men' might be dismissed as an admittedly factual but nonetheless untestable metaphysical statement. The studies in genetics just mentioned, however, indicate that such expressions may be given a quite hard and very testable scientific interpretation, one much harder to dismiss.

Although to demonstrate that there may be logical relations

15

between factual and normative statements is important, it is just as important not to overestimate or overinterpret what has been shown. I have not shown that *all* moral statements are empirically falsifiable, only that *some* are. And even when we are concerned solely with those which *are* empirically falsifiable, I see no point in drawing from this information certain conclusions about the nature or character of these moral but empirically falsifiable assertions. For instance, I do not in any event accept the suggestion that empirical testability is the hallmark of a scientific theory, and I would under no circumstances wish to grant that falsifiable counsels of perfection are scientific statements![8]

2 The Reduction of Religion to Morality

Thus, in Victorian England, we find that the apostles of progress, having swept their churches clean of sacraments, altars, priests and pulpits, leaving nothing save a bare structure of ethical assertions, returned to curtained, cushioned, upholstered homes in which every sort of buried sexual superstition, traditionalist tyranny and emotional cant served as covering for dirty unswept corners and nameless secular filth.

Quentin Bell: *Bloomsbury* (p. 28)[1]

I

In another book, *The Retreat to Commitment*, I treated a version of our third possibility: that religion is reducible to morality.[1] There I argued that one such position – represented by what was known as Protestant liberalism – was quite convincing for a long period during the nineteenth century, but that it was decisively undermined by biblical exegesis as well as by philosophical and social criticism during the early decades of the twentieth century. I have just referred to this position as a *version* of our third possibility, and the qualifier should be taken seriously. For one thing, it is doubtful that Protestant liberalism did ever achieve a full reduction of religion to morality. For another, the defeat of Protestant liberalism was carried out within a Christian framework. That no reduction of religion to morality could be carried out within Christianity by no means implies that there is *no* religion which may not be reducible to morality. Confucianism is a possible candidate example of such a reduction.

We shall return to Protestant liberalism later, when our fifth alternative – the conflict between morality and religion – is considered. There would, however, be little point in discussing again here what I have already written about at length in *The Retreat to Commitment*, and I refer the interested reader to that book for my views on that matter. Nor can I discuss Confucianism or other Eastern religions here, not for lack of interest, but for want of space.

Rather, I shall centre my attention on the curious half-life existence that the attempt to assimilate religion to morality has led amongst certain British and American philosophers in recent years. I have in mind the sort of approach represented by R. B. Braithwaite's well-known study, *An Empiricist's View of the Nature of Religious Belief*.[1] This choice is not altogether fortunate; for whereas Protestant liberalism and the movements and ideas associated with it were lively and interesting phenomena, Braithwaite's approach – which one might think to call a debased late form of Protestant liberalism – is constructed on naïve and uninformed historical scholarship and philosophical analysis. It has to be discussed, however, because of its quite considerable influence; it is a sad truth about the philosophy of religion that some philosophers do not apply to it the same high analytical standards that they presumably employ when engaged in symbolic logic or in the analysis of science.

II

Braithwaite's chief concern was with the meaning of religious expressions, and his problem was set by the early logical empiricist criterion of meaning – which had much influenced him in his youth – according to which only those utterances had meaning which could be empirically verified or else were truths of logic. Braithwaite adopts a move common amongst post-war quondam logical empiricists. Without going so far as to state bluntly that the empiricist criterion of meaning is incorrect, Braithwaite is bold enough to suggest that it is not sufficient, and suggests that when one approaches certain subjects, such as morality and religion, one may study meaning in terms of the way assertions are *used* in these areas, without worrying about whether they may be verified in the ways required by early logical empiricists. Claiming that the meaning of any statement will be given by the way it is used, Braithwaite sets out to explain how religious statements are used by those who express their religious convictions thereby.

Without giving away any secrets about how he got there, Braithwaite quickly comes to the conclusion that religious assertions are used primarily as moral assertions and may thus be 'assimilated' to moral assertions. Like moral statements, religious statements are not scientifically verifiable; but they do nonetheless have a use: to wit, they express 'conative intentions'. A moral assertion expresses the intention of its asserter to act in a particular sort of way. The primary use of religious assertions is the same: religious assertions, within the context of the religious system within which they appear, are declarations of adherence to a policy of action or way of life or pattern of behaviour.

There is, however, Braithwaite continues, an important but subordinate sense in which religious assertions may differ somewhat from some moral assertions. Namely, religious assertions, unlike moral assertions, will be accompanied by particular stories. These stories will, at least in Christianity as interpreted by Braithwaite, be drawn from the Christian tradition, and they will help support an 'agapeistic' policy of behaviour.[4] The difference between agapeistic behaviour patterns as recommended by Christians and exactly the same behaviour patterns as recommended by proponents of other, non-Christian, religions, such as Judaism and Buddhism, will be that in the case of Christians one set of stories will be borne in mind; in the case of Jews, another set of stories borne in mind; in the case of Buddhists, yet another set of stories borne in mind, and so on. It is not at all necessary, on Braithwaite's account, for the asserter of a religious assertion to believe that the story he tells is true; he 'entertains' the story mentally in order to help him – psychologically, causally – to follow a pattern of behaviour which he might otherwise resist. Braithwaite notes that he has chosen the word 'story' as the most neutral word he could think of, and allows that other writers whom he admires, such as Matthew Arnold, have used words like 'parable', 'fairy-tale', 'allegory', 'fable', 'tale', 'myth', and so on to express a comparable idea. All of which brings us to this definition of the professing Christian: 'A man is not, I think, a professing Christian,' Braithwaite writes, 'unless he both proposes to live according to Christian moral principles and associates his intention with thinking of Christian stories; but he need not believe that the empirical propositions presented by the stories correspond to empirical fact.'[5]

The only remarkable thing about Braithwaite's account of religion is that it has been taken seriously by several dis-

19

tinguished philosophical writers. In the issues of the *Cambridge Review* devoted to discussion of Braithwaite's essay, J. N. Schofield, to be sure, made no secret of his poor opinion of Braithwaite's lecture. But Professor D. M. MacKinnon and Ian Ramsey, Bishop of Durham, treated it with respect, MacKinnon even describing it as a stimulating contribution to the philosophy of religion for which one should be grateful.[6] Amongst other writers, Professor John Macquarrie has written that Braithwaite gives 'quite a plausible analysis of religious language',[7] although several pages later in the same book Macquarrie writes that Braithwaite has 'surely exaggerated his thesis beyond what is plausible'.[8] Macquarrie's position is, then, unclear. On the other hand, we find Mr Renford Bambrough writing that Braithwaite's study 'is the most philosophically sophisticated of numerous recent writings in the same vein'.[9]

Part of the explanation for the attention paid to Braithwaite's contribution to the philosophy of religion may have been the perhaps inevitable association of this essay with a Cambridge event, namely: the conversion of Braithwaite to Christianity. One journalist, reporting the reminiscences of a Cambridge don, wrote of this:

> There has always been a touch of King's College religion about Cambridge – the very beautiful King's Chapel, with its very beautiful choir, where anyone, religious or not, would like to go to church – which means a touch of intellectualism and eccentricity. For instance, Richard Braithwaite, who is a professor of Moral Philosophy here, was persuaded – philosophically – to become a Christian in his adult life, but, apparently, only after an exchange of several letters between him and the church. He certainly behaved as though a private treaty had been made, with a table of exemptions for him, and everyone in Cambridge believed that this was so. When he was baptized, practically everybody who was anybody in Cambridge was there, except Wittgenstein.[10]

III

One difficulty readers of Braithwaite's pamphlet have had is to determine just what he meant. His key words, such as 'agapeistic', are so vague that it is difficult to know what might or might not count as such behaviour. Although Braithwaite has, in the course of replying to some of his critics, specified some of the things that he did not mean – such as a 'general policy of benevolence' – what he did mean remains unclear.

So let us adopt as an experiment Braithwaite's own proposal: that the meaning of an expression is to be found in its *use* – in order to determine what Braithwaite himself may, by his own definition, have meant. How does Braithwaite treat his own rule – or philosophical behaviour policy – that the meaning of an expression is to be found in its use? To be more specific, what does he mean when he indicates that the meaning of a Christian religious assertion is to be found in its use? Does he mean that its meaning is to be determined by the way in which Christians have traditionally used it? Or by the ways in which they use religious assertions today? No: neither of these is even considered. Rather, we find that the rule that Braithwaite is following is this: *The meaning of a Christian religious assertion is to be determined by the use that I (Braithwaite) make of it.* There is a rapid *unvoiced* transition from *the* use to *my* use, from the definite article to the personal pronoun.

Earlier Protestant liberalism had been undermined when historical biblical exegesis uncovered the *falsity* of the liberal portrait of Jesus, a portrait deeply permeated by a wrong interpretation of the Sermon on the Mount. Thousands of Protestant liberals soberly abandoned their Christian affiliations because they could not accept what appeared really to have been the 'Christian ethic' as objectively determined by biblical scholarship.

For Braithwaite such considerations as what the 'Christian ethic', i.e., the morality preached by Jesus of Nazareth, really may be are beside the point. Not only is the truth of the stories which he uses to prop up his agapeistic policies unimportant to him; it is apparently of no importance to him whether whatever stories he *finds* in the Christian tradition, or imagines to be there, are really there at all. He writes (p. 63):

Since different people will take different views as to what these fundamental moral principles are, the typical meaning of religious assertions will be different for different people. I myself take the typical meaning of the body of Christian assertions as being given by their proclaiming intentions to follow an agapeistic way of life, and for a description of this way of life – a description in general and metaphorical terms, but an empirical description nevertheless – I should quote most of the Thirteenth Chapter of I Corinthians. Others may think that the Christian way of life should be described somewhat differently, and will therefore take the typical meaning of the assertions of Christianity to correspond to their different view of its fundamental moral teaching.

Again, Braithwaite writes of the stories which are to be used to prop up moral behaviour: 'The empirical story-statements will vary from Christian to Christian; the doctrines of Christianity are capable of different empirical interpretations, and Christians will differ in the interpretations they put upon the doctrines' (p. 66). And at the very close of his essay, Braithwaite concludes, with certainty, that 'it is of the very essence of the Christian religion' that the questions 'What shall I do?' and 'What moral principles should I adopt?' *must be answered by each man for himself.*

In brief, for Braithwaite the very essence of the Christian religion is a subjective – arbitrary – choice of moral principles. Or might one say: *The very essence of Christianity is doing whatever you choose provided that you decorate whatever you choose to do with stories from the Christian tradition which you may interpret in any way you please.*

This is, however, preposterous as an interpretation of the Christian tradition *as it is used*; it is a quixotic and eccentric legislative proposal on Braithwaite's part about how the Christian tradition might be used. If it were true that nothing more could be found in Christianity save a few moral homilies, Braithwaite might indeed be doing Christians a small service by championing such a use, however little it had to do with the tradition. But this is clearly not the case. His lip service to science to the contrary, Braithwaite ignores the objective findings of scientific historical biblical scholarship when he defines the essence of Christianity as agapeistic behaviour.

This is hardly the place to expound what the Christian tradition really is. Better perhaps to insist that there may well be no such thing as the essence of Christianity, to urge that

Christianity is made up of a multitude of different and conflicting policies, stories, doctrines, and also of scientific and metaphysical assertions. There are, to be sure, parts of the tradition that stress what one might translate into something of the sort that Braithwaite evidently means by agapeistic behaviour – the thirteenth chapter of I Corinthians (which Braithwaite cites), the first epistle of John, or (when taken out of context) the Sermon on the Mount. But to concentrate on these is quite arbitrary. Anyone might of course say that one particular strand of the Christian tradition appeals to him more than another. But there is a logical leap from 'I find such and such an aspect of Christianity appealing' to 'I am a Christian'. If one finds some aspect of Buddhism appealing is one then a Buddhist too?

Nor does it help, as Braithwaite appears to think it may, to say that seemingly conflicting parts of the tradition will support an agapeistic interpretation if put into context. One might as well argue that a different claim which some have advanced – namely, that Christianity is essentially a prudential ethic – would also be borne out if put into context. By picking and choosing, one can find biblical backing and context for dozens of different behavioural policies.

It can be instructive, if we really do want to put agapeistic accounts of Christianity such as Braithwaite's into context, to ask what Christians pray for. How many prayers in the Book of Common Prayer ask for support in agapeistic behaviour? Very few. Quite the contrary, prayers tend to ask for protection against dangers and enemies. The second Collect, for Peace, in the service for Morning Prayer reads:

> O God, who art the author of peace and lover of concord, in knowledge of whom standeth our eternal life, whose service is perfect freedom; Defend us thy humble servants in all assaults of our enemies; that we, surely trusting in thy defence, may not fear the power of any adversaries, through the might of Jesus Christ our Lord.

And for what does one pray at night? The second Collect at Evening Prayer reads:

> O God, from whom all holy desires, all good counsels, and all just works do proceed; Give unto thy servants that

peace which the world cannot give; that both our hearts may be set to obey thy commandments, and also that by thee we being defended from the fear of our enemies may pass our time in rest and quietness.

And one of the most famous of all prayers, the beautiful prayer of St Chrysostom reads:

Almighty God, who hast given us grace at this time with one accord to make our common supplications unto thee; and dost promise, that when two or three are gathered together in thy Name thou wilt grant their requests: Fulfil now, O Lord, the desires and petitions of thy servants, as may be most expedient for them; granting us in this world knowledge of thy truth, and in the world to come life everlasting.

Or ought one to consider the Creed of St Athanasius, also in the Book of Common Prayer, and although not much used in contemporary times, directed nonetheless to be recited in place of the Apostles' Creed on Christmas Day, the Epiphany, Easter Day, Ascension Day, Whitsunday, Trinity Sunday, and on the Feast Days of eight of the saints? It is very long, and wears the dress of a philosophical terminology long obsolete. I shall quote only from the beginning and the end:

Whosoever will be saved: before all things it is necessary that he hold the Catholick Faith. Which Faith except everyone do keep *whole and undefiled*: without doubt he shall perish everlastingly. And the Catholick Faith is this: That we worship one God in Trinity, and Trinity in Unity; Neither confounding the Persons; nor dividing the Substance. . . .

And so on for four columns of very small print. *Not a single word is said of love*, not a single word in this great creed of the Church which ends in these words: 'This is the Catholick Faith: which except a man believe faithfully, he cannot be saved.' For that matter, there is not a word about love in the Apostles' Creed, the most widely used creed of the Christian churches. Why? Part of the answer seems to be that the creeds were intended in part to define heresies to be avoided, and to pronounce on matters over which there had been some disagreement in the

24

early history of the church. That Christ preached some vague gospel of love has rarely been contested – *so* vague that there were few doctrinal disputes about it; and also, I fear, so *uninteresting* to the majority of Christians, that it was not considered necessary to incorporate a reference to it in the creeds. What was wanted was protection against dangers: give us that, dear God, and we may even do some loving.

But if there were in the early centuries of the church few doctrinal disputes about love, historical scholarship has had something to say about it. One result of nineteenth-century biblical criticism was that the Sermon on the Mount, which many took as the paradigm statement of Jesus's gospel of love, was not at all meant as a general policy of behaviour even for Christians but was rather what Albert Schweitzer called an interim ethic, a prudential ethic to be followed by a small group of Christians isolated from general society expecting the imminent return of a God who would protect them from the dangers of that society and indeed set them up as lords over it.[11] To this topic I shall return in the next chapter.

Braithwaite's account of Christianity is, then, somewhat simple-minded. The same may be said of his view of literature in general: for Braithwaite, the chief function of Christian stories is, like that of myths, parables and other kinds of literature, to give us causal fodder to bolster our moral intentions. The function of literature, and in particular the question whether it is morally uplifting or morally degrading, has been discussed by philosophers and critics from Plato to F. R. Leavis – with many rather different conclusions. It is perhaps worth remarking that one important thing that may happen when one confronts great literature is that one's perceptions may be heightened and changed by the artistic and imaginative presentation of possible human situations. Literature does not simply strengthen one's moral resolutions; and it would on any account be superficial to say that this is *the* function of literature. Literature has no single function and has in fact been used for many different purposes in the course of its history. Few who have read such writers as Marcel Proust, Robert Musil, Richard Hughes, Virginia Woolf, E. M. Forster, have failed to be both affected and *changed* by the encounter. Sometimes, of course, material from this literature may be used to help support one's previous moral resolutions; but just as often it may have an

25

effect – at once destructive and constructive – of altering radically one's moral resolutions.

IV

It would be wrong to leave this topic before discussing in somewhat broader connexion some of the ideas and expressions that we have been using, such as 'religious assertions' and 'religious language'. Some philosophers are regrettably wont to talk of something called 'religious language' as if it were a unique category of discourse, quite separate from other such categories as 'historical narrative', 'scientific explanation', 'poetry', 'symbolic discourse', 'allegory', 'myth', and several other ways and modes of speaking. A detailed review of the reasons for taking, and rejecting, this approach, however interesting, is not needed here. Suffice it to say that such accounts of 'religious language', so-called, tend to begin with the intention of marking it off as one of a number of *illegitimate* forms of discourse to be distinguished from one or two legitimate forms of discourse – such as formal logic and mathematics on one hand and scientific explanation on the other. Logical empiricism is one example of such an approach. Later, as this logical and scientific imperialism was being abandoned, some philosophers – Braithwaite is a good example – persisted in speaking of 'religious language', but dropped the earlier pejorative tone. Now 'religious language' was to be construed as something with properties all its own, even its own unique criteria in terms of which religious statements could be validated or rejected. These thinkers would sometimes maintain that just as there could be developed a logic of scientific discourse, or a logic of scientific discovery, so there could be developed a logic of religious discourse – neither of which could be judged in terms of the criteria held valid by any of the others.

The results of contemporary investigations in philosophy, philology, linguistics, anthropology, comparative religion and other fields provide little support for either of these approaches. Language is used importantly in religion, but there is no such thing as 'religious language', any more than there is a single thing, 'Religion', which has a kind of language appropriate and peculiar to it: there are many different religions, each

26

with their own distinctive styles of discourse; and even within a particular religion, such as Christianity, many different kinds of language are used. There is the rich poetic language, filled with metaphor and hyperbole, simile, allusion, of the Psalms or the Song of Solomon. There is the comparatively straightforward historical narrative of much of the Books of Samuel and Kings and of Joshua, or again, of the Gospels and the Book of the Acts of the Apostles. There are at one extreme the letters of Paul, occasionally bordering on the ordinary, and at the other extreme the altogether extraordinary language of the Book of Revelations. Also to be mentioned are the various prayer books and liturgies, the hymns of the churches, and the oral traditions. So, we may speak of the languages of religions, or of the language of religions; but we begin to go astray if we think that there is something which might be called 'religious language' or that there is a category of assertions that can easily be pigeonholed as 'religious assertions'. There is no 'language of religion' which could be studied exhaustively like, say, the language of the Hopi Indians during a particular decade; nor is there a category of religious assertions which could be studied intensively like an axiom system of symbolic logic or mathematics. One very great theologian, Karl Barth, did say that the *Word of God* (which is not to be identified with any human report of it) could not appropriately have the criteria of disciplines other than theology brought in judgement upon it. But even theological criteria remained hypothetical for Barth; and he would have scoffed at the idea of 'religious language'.[12]

V

Having made these remarks about the language of religions, I hope that no reader will make the mistake of supposing that what I have to say about religion and language in the following applies to all religions or even to all language within any particular religion. Nor do I want to suggest that what I am about to say about religious language can be true *only* of religious language. Quite the contrary: there are political, and even scientific systems of thought in which similar things can happen.

27

Nonetheless, I hope to concentrate on certain things that can happen to language when we are careless, and which appear to happen with peculiar frequency in the languages of religions. I shall dwell on the dangers of religious discourse – without thereby implying that discourse in other areas is notably safer.

Some eminent theologians – Rudolf Bultmann, Reinhold Niebuhr, Paul Tillich are examples – have been struck by two things: they have been worried about the obscurity and seeming irrelevance to contemporary problems of much traditional religious language. And they have, as biblical scholars and theologians, been especially sensitive to the immense riches of the Christian heritage – the *entire* heritage, not, like Braithwaite, only a tiny segment of it. Tillich, for example, noticing that some traditional Christian concepts – such as that of original sin, which can be explicated in psychological terms – have not outworn their usefulness, took as one of his tasks to restate and redefine such concepts, with the hope of eliminating their supernatural features and of bringing their still valuable aspects into better focus. 'You must first save concepts,' he once wrote, 'before you can save souls.' In his various books and essays, he analysed various human problems confronting contemporary persons, and attempted to show that particular biblical themes can provide, when reinterpreted, important insights into these problems. Grace, redemption, transformation, these – as well as particular stories, such as that of the dying God, the heroic saviour – can, when 'demythologised' in the light of Tillichian or Bultmannian scrutiny, aid in the care and cure of contemporary neuroses and other difficulties. Although one may quarrel in detail with Niebuhr, Tillich, Bultmann and others who have tried such approaches, one can hardly object to the general approach. The Bible is after all rich in wisdom. Moreover, the writers just mentioned differ from Braithwaite in several important respects, two of those most relevant here being that they were never logical empiricists and that their knowledge both of biblical and other literature is too wide to permit them to reduce Christianity to a morality coloured and reinforced by a particular tale.

An important difficulty, however, arises when the demythologised material rendered by these theologians is used in

apologetic defence of an exclusively Christian orientation. For
other faiths, not to mention literature, such as Greek tragedy
and Shakespeare – and the novels of Dostoevsky and Bunyan
of which Braithwaite made mention – also contain symbols and
myths embodying important insight about the way men might
confront life-situations. At the moment I am writing these
words, hundreds of copies of the latest edition or re-edition of
the *I Ching* – an ancient Chinese book of moral and religious
wisdom which, despite its common use as a magic oracle, ranks
with the greatest religious texts – are being bought by young
people in England and America.[13] The Indian tales which
Heinrich Zimmer so ably popularised, such as 'Die Geschichte
vom indischen König mit dem Leichnam', and 'Abu Kasems
Pantoffeln', when published in paperback in English quickly
went out of print.[14] And the late David Stacton's novel
Kaliyuga, an extraordinary work, was directly influenced by
Zimmer's researches.[15] These are only a few examples,
taken from relatively popular literature, to illustrate two simple
points: (1) religions other than Christianity possess symbols and
myths embodying important truths about the way men might
confront life, *and* (2) this material is being used by thousands of
Westerners of Christian background daily. What then is to
preserve any claim of Christianity to religious superiority? What
is to mark off the 'true faith' of Christianity from competing
faiths? Interestingly, Paul Tillich, during the final years of his
life, under the influence of studies in comparative religion made
by Mircea Eliade and others, began to retreat from his own
earlier Christian exclusivism.

VI

Yet another problem to be faced is that despite the worthy
intentions of the biblical reconstructionists, their programmes
have backfired, become self-defeating, because they have
led to a profound breakdown of communication amongst
Christians. One source of the breakdown of communication is
a tendency to fit traditional doctrines to new situations by
redefining the words in which the doctrines are phrased. The
traditional doctrines become counters in an elaborate game.
'To be a Christian' begins to resemble 'to go dancing'. All that

29

is needed of a couple dancing is that they both know and follow the rules. They need agree about no substantial issue: neither about morals, politics, art nor science. A bitterly quarrelling married couple may still *enjoy* dancing – or, *pace* Freud, sexual intercourse – together; such may remain activities in which they can co-operate whilst leaving their many disagreements unspoken. But are two such people truly communicating?

Or, in the case of two Christians who agree about little substantial but who in religious services both know when to say the proper phrases and when and how to carry out the appropriate actions together – are *they* communicating? They too are doubtless co-operating – and doing so in what an external obsereer might interpret as an agapeistic pattern of behaviour. Yet satisfactory communication with a person presumably involves appreciation of what *he* means when he says such things as: 'I believe in God', 'Jesus Christ is Lord', or 'God is love'.

By carelessness in the use of language, theologians run the risk of debasing the rich linguistic heritage of the Christian tradition. Suppose that one's language has become so debased that one can no longer tell when one is disagreeing with the person with whom one is talking. Communication demands that both parties be able to find out in what respects they disagree: two people cannot understand each other if they have no way of determining when they disagree. Yet 'word-healing' and the ceremonial use of language, as often practised in contemporary theology, make it difficult for contemporary Christians to ascertain when they are disagreeing about religious questions. To the extent to which articulation of disagreement ceases to occur, to the extent to which what I call the 'indiscernibility of disagreement' prevails, any kind of communication, including that religious communication which is supposed to possess saving power, falters.

VII

It is worthwhile to place these polemical remarks about religious language in the broader context of the theory of language, with especial attention to Karl Bühler's famous book

Sprachtheorie, first published in 1934 in Leipzig, and recently republished.[16] Bühler analysed the communicative function of a language into three components: (1) *the expressive function*, where the communication serves to express the emotions or thoughts of the speaker; (2) the *signalling* or *stimulative* or *release function*: that is, the communication serves to stimulate or to release certain reactions in the hearer; (3) *the descriptive function*, which is present to the extent that the communication describes some state of affairs. These three functions are separable in so far as each is accompanied by its preceding one but need not be accompanied by its succeeding one. That is, one may express without signalling; one may express and signal without describing. But one cannot signal without expressing, or describe without both expressing and signalling. Yet another function has been added to Bühler's set: namely, *the argumentative function*, to which the same hierarchical ordering applies: one cannot argue without describing, signalling, expressing.[17] The first two functions apply, of course, to animal languages. Animals surely do express and signal. But the second two functions, describing and arguing about those descriptions, may possibly be characteristically human — although those who research into the life and languages of animals may well hope for discoveries which will refute at least some of our views about the limitations of animal communication. There is, for instance, some sense in which bees describe.

As an aid in the understanding of his ideas, Bühler developed the diagram below.[18]

The triangle in the middle denotes the linguistic *sign*. This sign may be used by the sender or sqeaker to exqress himself; it may be received by the receiver or listener as a signal or appeal which may or may not have been intended by the speaker. And the same sign again may be used — by sender, receiver, or both — to symbolise some objective state of affairs independent of the receiver and sender. An application of the scheme to contemporary art, music and poetry can be very instructive. Extend the sign beyond conventional language to such things as works of art. A work of art may express certain subjective states of mind or intentions on the part of the artist; those who receive or respond to the work of art may or may not decode it as it was intended by its original sender. And the work of art may or may not be representational. To co-ordinate various

31

contemporary theories and modes of artistic expression with Bühler's schema is an exercise both instructive and amusing.

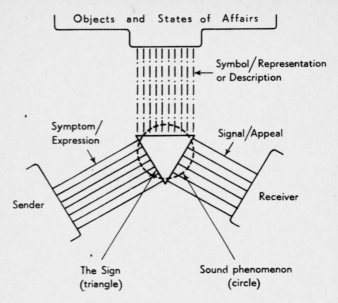

If we look fairly at the history of religion, rather than at art, to determine how these comments about language apply, we find the following. Despite the attacks of logical empiricists who would permit religious expressions at best an emotive meaning, and the views of such as Braithwaite who would assimilate religious assertions to signalling and appeal policies for moral behaviour – things able to be analysed roughly in terms of Bühler's first two functions – it can hardly be doubted that religious discourse was in its origins often intended to be descriptive and explanatory as well as expressive and stimulative, and that this remains true today. Moreover, the history of religion is full of quite genuine and often rigorous arguments about the truth of these explanations and descriptions.

This heritage is in danger of being lost today; religious discourse is in danger of being reduced – as if this were a favour to religion! – to the first two functions. Ironically, perhaps the most serious danger of this happening comes from the attempts of theologians, no doubt just as well-intentioned as Braithwaite, but misguided and even eccentric for all that, to defend religion.

32

I have already mentioned how the very coin of religious discourse may be debased by excessive ambiguity of meanings. It is worth mentioning another self-defeating strategy to which the Bühler schema is particularly relevant.

Some theologians – Reinhold Niebuhr is an example – have suggested that human logic is responsible for having led us into difficulties in trying to comprehend and defend religious doctrine, and have recommended that instead of trying to reconcile seemingly contradictory doctrines we instead abandon logic, together with its laws of non-contradiction and *tertium non datur*. Now logic has a way of avenging herself on those who treat her lightly. *If we abandon logic, we lose the power of argument*: for argument consists, in essence, in showing that two claims are incompatible. *And if we abandon logic we also diminish enormously our powers of description*: for to say what something is, to describe it, is at the same time to say a great deal about what it is not. And if we allow contradictions to be introduced, we permit all descriptions at once. Thus one defensive move – the scuttling of logic – forces us step by step down the hierarchy of linguistic functions. We lose the power to argue, we lose the power to describe; we are left with the powers to express and to signal. Such may be sufficient in poetry. It may be sufficient in, say, music. There can be no doubt that the expressive and stimulative functions of our various languages are by themselves alone astonishingly rich and deep. But are they rich and deep enough, do they suffice, for religion? Or do they debase and emasculate it? Some persons, like myself, who sympathise with the rich heritage of traditional Christianity even though we are critical of it, would wish that more theologians could keep these elementary linguistic considerations in mind during their defences of religion. It is at least conceivable that their cures are worse than the disease. Moreover, these cures are infectious and may spread to areas other than religion. For example, historical writing and political argument may be debased by tactics similar to those used unintentionally to debase religious discourse.

The ambiguities of language are great gifts – and great dangers.

3 Morality and Religion in Conflict

> Nothing can come of converting the question about duty and
> right, about the moral subject, into the question about the
> reality and practical possibilities of man as the object of our
> thought – as if man himself as such were not called in
> question by the consideration of what ought to be.
>
> Karl Barth: *The Word of God and the Word of Man*
> (p. 137)

I

Since we are concerned principally with the question of the
interdependence of morality and religion, we need not occupy
ourselves with the fourth case mentioned at the beginning of
this study: namely, that in which morality and religion are
fully compatible, but in which neither is reducible to the other.
In the fourth case morality and religion are consistent – and
independent.

Rather, we may proceed at once to the fifth case, in which
morality is not derivable from religion or vice versa; and where
the two conflict to at least some extent but not wholly. Of many
writings on such conflict, the most influential in recent years
have probably been those of Søren Kierkegaard and Karl
Barth.

In turning to the thought of Kierkegaard we appear to be
leaving twentieth-century thought for the first time in this
study, and to be backtracking to the nineteenth century. The
appearance is, however, deceptive. Kierkegaard stood quite
apart from most religious writers of his own time and until his
thought suddenly became relevant – during the second decade
of the twentieth century – his influence was marginal. Chiefly
responsible for bringing Kierkegaard's thought to public notice
at this time were three writers: the Danish philosopher, Harald
Höffding; the German, Theodor Haecker, whose work on
Kierkegaard (1913) influenced Karl Kraus and Martin Buber
in Vienna and certain members of the Brenner Kreis around
Ludwig von Ficker in Innsbruck; and most important, the
Swiss theologian Karl Barth. Here we can discuss only the

relationship between the thought and situations of Kierkegaard
and Barth.

II

In his book *The Epistle to the Romans*, first published in 1918[1] –
the book that made his reputation and is often credited with
having started the neo-orthodox movement in Protestantism –
Barth quoted Kierkegaard generously; and for the following
eight years – until Kierkegaard's ideas began to be put to uses
of which Barth did not approve[2] – he made no secret of his
immense debt to him.

In Kierkegaard Barth found a natural predecessor and ally.
For Kierkegaard had already avoided in the 1840s the main
snare in which liberal Protestants found themselves caught by
the beginning of the World War; and he had taken the alternate
approach to theological questions which their main opponents
and successors, led by Barth, were to follow.

Kierkegaard's chief problem had been: 'What does it mean
to be a Christian?' The question had not only been asked
before; controversies over problems of defining the essence of
Christianity or of 'being a Christian' had troubled Christian
writers from the earliest days of the church. By Kierkegaard's
time, however, an impregnable answer to the question was
becoming increasingly urgent.

Only a generation before Kierkegaard reached maturity,
Immanuel Kant, after having given a shattering blow to
traditional theology and metaphysics, and an incisive critique
of the proofs for the existence of God, aligned himself with those
who located the essence of Christianity in its morality. By the
time Kierkegaard had begun to write, Protestant liberalism,
which was to be closely associated throughout its history with
neo-Kantianism, had fully emerged as an effort to show that
the essence of Christian doctrine, construed as its moral
teaching, harmonised with modern progressive cultural
thinking, and that nothing hence prevented a reasonable
modern man from affiliating himself with it. Here Protestant
liberalism followed a well-established tendency. Throughout
Protestant intellectual history it had been widely though not
consistently assumed that the results of independent scientific

36

inquiry would tally, when properly interpreted, with Protestant teaching. The alliance was to be sure an on-again, off-again affair, but sufficed to permit scientists and Protestant theologians to mount a common front against Roman Catholic obscurantism on one hand and the fundamentalism of some of the working-class Protestant sects on the other hand. In practice, the dominance of the scientific side of this alliance led to a steady erosion of Protestant teaching. The importance of the celebrated controversies over geological discoveries and Darwin has been exaggerated. In fact, the more eminent Protestant theologians discarded the Bible's cosmological and scientific statements relatively painlessly. For by Darwin's time, they had grown used to the idea of a refurbished Christianity, independent of many features of traditional Christianity, such as the sort of natural theology that was dependent on those very proofs for the existence of a deity which Kant and others had discredited. All these, it was insisted, were transient, accidental accretions on Christian doctrine: the essence of Jesus's teaching was the Christian ethic, as exemplified in the Sermon on the Mount.

Particularly important to this ethic, and especially relevant to an understanding of Kierkegaard, is Kant's universalisability principle, according to which an argument against an act such as murder might go as follows: 'One ought not to do that, for if everyone were to do that the results would be catastrophic. Therefore no one should do that.' A reasonable moral objection to a proposed act would, then, be that it could not be universalised.

Many nineteenth-century Protestant theologians did work within such a Kantian approach, particularly as it was developed by followers of Hegel. Having shelved the various biblical cosmologies and Aristotelian metaphysics, they argued that a morality lay at the core of Jesus's teaching. Accordingly, much biblical criticism of this period was oriented towards reconstructing the life of the historical Jesus so as to depict him as a good, eminently reasonable, nineteenth-century Danish or German liberal Lutheran bishop, after whose life one might well pattern one's own. Could not the Sermon on the Mount, with its injunction: 'Do unto others as ye would have them do unto you', be read as a kind of anticipation of Kant's universalisability principle? Hegel, for instance, appears to

37

have toyed with this idea in his early essay 'The Life of Jesus' (1795). Within an approach which took the historical Jesus as a paradigm example of a good rational social manager or reformer, liberal Protestant Christianity could be presented as a most reasonable form of belief because interpretations of its personal and social ethics (presumably based on those of Jesus) seemed in harmony with the rationalist ethics of Kant, Hegel and their followers.

Kierkegaard, standing apart from his contemporaries, wrote scathing denunciations of this wordly 'ethical Christianity' and the presumed marriage between rationalism and Protestantism which he thought responsible for it. A recurring theme in his writing is that Christendom lacks character. It is easy to be a Christian: so-called Christians neither accept nor reject Christianity seriously – and thus do not take it seriously. If some tenet were attacked by reason, the tenet would be rejected or reinterpreted. Reason marched forward conquering new ground; Christendom followed dutifully after. If this were to continue, Kierkegaard warned, Christianity stood in danger of losing its claim to distinctiveness. In *Fear and Trembling* Kierkegaard allows his pseudonymous author, Johannes de Silentio, to comment that the Greeks could have done just as much so far as ethics was concerned: no revelation, nothing special was required. And for this reason, such a limited form of Christianity stood in danger of losing its identity. Kierkegaard thought that the picture of Jesus as a great practical moral teacher – even if correct – would have been both insufficient and inappropriate as a defence of Christianity. *But what if it were undermined by historical scholarship instead of reinforced by it*? What would be left? Kierkegaard's question was terribly prescient. For by the first decade of the present century this picture of the historical Jesus had come to grief.

Indeed, in the decade prior to the publication of Barth's *Epistle to the Romans* the Protestant liberals suffered a most extraordinary and ironical reverse. Although the liberals themselves had sponsored the ambitious programme of biblical exegesis conducted during the nineteenth century, and in particular the 'quest for the historical Jesus', their own historical researches proved to discredit their own image of the historical Jesus. Jesus, it turned out, had not preached a liberal ethical creed. Schweitzer and other biblical scholars argued that

38

when set in its historical context the Sermon on the Mount had to be read as an interim ethic, not designed for a practical politics of love but for a brief period between the crucifixion and an imminent Last Judgement. Jesus himself appeared to be a forbidding, world-denying figure, hardly a nineteenth-century-style social reformer with whom Protestants could easily identify.

In brief, what had been called the Christian ethic by many Christians during the nineteenth century was – just as Kierkegaard had warned – not Christian. The Christian ethic was no more essential to Christianity than was the Christian cosmology. To be sure, Kierkegaard himself rarely discussed nineteenth-century, ethics-oriented biblical criticism directly; and from the few comments he did make one can tell that he hardly anticipated all the results which Schweitzer records – not to mention later twentieth-century research. Nonetheless, there are passages in *Fear and Trembling* which are clearly meant to mock the *Leben Jesu* of David Strauss, an important biblical scholar of the nineteenth century. And in *Training in Christianity* and *The Philosophical Fragments*, Kierkegaard clearly denies the apologetic effectiveness of such historical research. 'History', Kierkegaard writes, 'makes out Christ to be another than he truly is.' Although Kierkegaard scoffed at the effectiveness of such historical research, he had a picture of the historical Jesus which differed sharply from that of the liberals.

Kierkegaard buttressed his attack on rational, ethics-centred Christianity with a direct defence of the 'absurd'. Using the familiar fideistic-sceptical arguments that one can find in Sextus Empiricus, in Pascal or in Bayle, Kierkegaard emphasised the essential incompleteness of any rationalistic system, for example Hegel's. In his *Concluding Unscientific Postscript*, *Philosophical Fragments*, *De Omnibus Dubitandum Est*, *Fear and Trembling*, *Training in Christianity* and elsewhere, he argued that rationality is necessarily limited, that the correctness of any system or way of life can never be proved. Any attempt to do so generates an infinite regress of proving; and, so he argued, a dogmatic presupposition is therefore necessary. To adopt any particular way of life one has to make an irrational existential choice of some 'absolute presupposition' or revelation. This act of choice will not be determined by any 'rational criterion' – such as the 'universalisability principle'. In effect, Kierkegaard argued

39

that there is an excuse for irrationalism against which a rationalist has no defence, since it is valid from his own point of view.

III

And here we arrive at the way in which the conflict between morality and religion is dramatised by Kierkegaard. If there is indeed such a limit to rationality, why should God not countermand a reasonable ethic? For instance, God could even demand murder through what Kierkegaard calls a 'teleological suspension of the ethical'. This very possibility Kierkegaard explores in *Fear and Trembling*, where Abraham demonstrates his *absurd* faith in God first by believing, contrary to familiar biological laws, that his wife Sarah would bear him a son in her old age; and then by his readiness to kill his beloved son Isaac at God's command in spite of the absurd violation of reasonable ethics which such an act would involve.

Kierkegaard concentrated on the Abraham story for many reasons. First, he probably knew that Kant had criticised Abraham's behaviour as unreasonable in his *The Quarrel Amongst the Faculties* (1798). Secondly, one might have expected a Christian writer like Kierkegaard to have chosen Jesus as his example of the man of faith. By contrast to many writers of his time, Kierkegaard avoided, particularly in his earlier work, pinning the essence of Christian action on the imitation of the historical Jesus. To be a man of faith was for him *to obey God* blindly, absurdly, without recourse to reason – one's model of the man of faith being more Abraham than Jesus.

This is not to say that Kierkegaard entirely avoided speaking of the imitation of Christ. Especially in the tenth volume of the Danish edition of *Søren Kierkegaards Papirer*, Kierkegaard does write, rather vaguely, of the imitation of Christ, usually stressing suffering, solitude, and renunciation of this world. This may well have been due to Kierkegaard's eventual reconciliation to the fact that he was not to marry or have a conventional career. But even in this later work Kierkegaard does not use the imitation of Christ for an apologetic purpose, and he elaborately qualifies his use of the word 'imitate'. Moreover, his conception of a world-renouncing historical Jesus, although erroneous in detail, is close to those of Schweitzer, Barth and

40

the neo-orthodox thinkers, and far removed from the liberal portrait.

IV

Consequently – and this is the point – the investigations into the character of the historical Jesus which eventually destroyed the many liberal portraits of Jesus as a great practical moral teacher hardly affected Kierkegaard's characterisation of the essence of being a Christian. Kierkegaard, having avoided the traps of late nineteenth-century theology and biblical scholarship which eventually shattered Protestant liberalism, suddenly became relevant, and loomed at the end of World War I as one of the few significant Christian thinkers of the nineteenth century who had not only not succumbed to Protestant liberalism, but who had attacked it in its heyday. Kierkegaard's appeal to the early Barth and his followers needs little further explanation.

V

We have taken Kierkegaard as a striking example of a writer who stresses not simply the existence of a conflict between morality and religion but even the necessity for one. His religious hero, Abraham, serves, within the Judeo-Christian tradition, as a paradigm example of the man *obedient* to God. When a conflict arises between his allegiance on the one hand to the moral code – indeed to what is understood to be God's own moral code, forbidding murder – and on the other hand to religious commandment which stands in stark disagreement with the moral code, the choice he must make is clear. In the Old Testament the agony of that choice is plainly illustrated; but just as plain is its inevitability. For Abraham there is an 'either/or'. Morality would bring him to one decision; obedience to God would bring him to another. As the man of faith he had to obey God.

Whatever Barth's later reservations about Kierkegaard or his influence may have been, Barth remains the contemporary

41

theologian most emphatic in stressing the same difference between – and possible conflict between – the Word of God and the Word of Man. In his later years, surveying the growing weakness of the Protestant churches, Barth wrote increasingly of the solitude and isolation of the theologian. Yet if he ever wavered in his own absolute commitment to what he called the Word of God, he did not – unlike Tillich – parade his doubting. 'There is no justification for doubt itself,' he insisted. 'No one should flirt with his unbelief or with his doubt. The theologian should only be sincerely *ashamed* of it.'[3] The italics are Barth's.

Yet it is not the familiar irrationally committed neo-Calvinist 'dogmatist' that I wish to emphasise here. I wish also to recall a side of Barth that is almost never mentioned. In fact, he was one of the most brilliant strategists of theological survival in the history of the Christian church. Far from being dogmatic in the ordinary sense of that word, he was remarkably flexible, a most rational irrationalist, one who was – reputation notwithstanding – not one whit more an irrationalist than, to pick arbitrarily on two well-known rationalists, Sir Alfred Ayer or Sir Karl Popper. And what makes it possible to say this of Barth is precisely his treatment of what he saw as the inescapable necessity for commitment involving a choice between morality and religion.

A man of regular habits, Barth listened to the music of Mozart for one half-hour each morning. Writing of Mozart, he characterised himself: 'This man was creative, even and precisely while he was imitating. Verily, he did not only imitate. From the beginning he moved freely within the frame of the rules of the art of his time, and later more and more freely. But he did not revolt against these rules, nor break them. He sought and found his greatness in remaining himself precisely while binding himself to these rules. One must see both his freedom and his restraint, side by side, and seek his singular quality behind this very riddle.'[4] Moving creatively within the rules was the problem, and the riddle, of Barth's own life.

His own solution to this riddle set the strategy for religious defence and renewal within Protestantism from the early 1920s until the late 1950s. The key to his solution is contained in two insights: first, only one of the rules was after all fundamental:

42

namely, that the Christian theologian be committed to the 'Word of God', as revealed in Jesus; second, as a corollary, the theologian ought not to commit himself to any particular interpretation of the Word of God, to any particular cultural morality or ideology; the church must not be permitted to become a mere reflection of social and cultural conditions, and it certainly was no servant of secular morality.

Since such talk often bewilders people, it may be helpful to try to explain it by mapping these expressions approximately into perfectly ordinary secular language. Take the case of the natural scientist: he is presumably committed to the truth about the natural world, but is not committed to the truth of any particular hypothesis about the nature of that natural world. Substitute 'theologian' for 'natural scientist', 'Word of God' for 'natural world', and 'interpretation' for 'hypothesis', and you have the crux of Barth's position.

But what is this 'Word of God'? That is indeed the question. Unlike the fundamentalists, Barth does not identify the Word of God with the Bible. Rather, even the Bible is taken by him to be one more interpretation or witness – a fallible witness – to the revelatory historical event which it is *assumed* that it reports. If this is so of the Bible, it is all the more so, in Barth's view, of all other theological statements, such as those in the Creeds, those made in sermons, those embodied in theological systems, those of the traditions and councils of the church. *All* are to be considered conjectural, subject to constant revision and testing against the Word of God itself. Thus the locus of religious authority is removed from the documents and utterances of the church to the historical event to which they purport to bear witness.

If the Word of God is to be treated thus, the job of the theologian is redefined accordingly. If by definition any theologian is committed to the Word of God, *argument on behalf of* it, e.g., traditional apologetic theology, is forbidden to him as useless and irreverent. The task of the theologian is restricted to: (1) description or exposition of the Word of God and (2) criticism and testing of his own and other descriptions, past and current. Thus *argument, creative discussion and disagreement, about the content* of the Word of God is required, even to be expected. *Argument about the truth* of the Word of God is however forbidden. Thus Barth bound himself, and yet remained creative.

43

Yet, to exclude argument about the truth of the Word of God is to adopt a minimal but nonetheless absolute concession to irrationalism: one that was indeed to form the basis for neo-orthodoxy. Asking not, 'What is the essence of Christianity?' but 'What is essential to being a Christian?', Barth demanded of Christians nothing more, or less, than absolute commitment to the Word of God as revealed by Jesus. The required commitment proved, in Barth's exposition, to be vague in a rather precise and quite convenient way. It was sufficiently vague to allow a flexibility amongst Protestant theologians surpassing even that of many of the old liberals. Never again was any identification of Christian doctrine with a fixed cultural viewpoint or ideology, whether liberal or Calvinist, to be permitted. On the other hand, the limits of this flexibility were defined, in that commitment to the Word of God was not itself subject to reconsideration.

The flexibility of Barth's formula enabled the ecumenical movement for union amongst Protestant churches to minimise the importance of the denominations' differing interpretations of Christian doctrine and to emphasise their common commitment to the Word of God. Since even the formula was open to different interpretations, the resulting flexibility was wide. In any case, Barth's formula was written into the constitutions of the new ecumenical organisations as the price of admission; and at the same time, by exacting this price, Protestants gained at least the illusion of taking a new tough-minded line. Their formula might indeed be so vague as to be virtually empty: but it was not susceptible to erosion by the latest findings of science or by cultural fads.

Moreover, Barth's emphasis on *searching* for the Word of God propped psychologically the Protestants' sagging morale by explaining the collapse of earlier statements about the true essence of Christianity, and providing explicitly for the possibility that even more radical revisions would take place in the future.

Barth's formula was of course not without its own dangers, ones with which he never satisfactorily dealt: if the character of the Jesus or the Word of God to whom assent was required was indefinite, and if such commitment was required *no matter*

44

what Jesus was and did, at best the subjective commitment itself would be definite. Its object would be an 'I know not what and I care not what' – perhaps a less than satisfactory object of worship.

VII

In view of Barth's critique of Protestant liberalism and his religious conservativism, one might expect him to have been politically reactionary. On the contrary, he was a socialist, and had once seriously contemplated devoting his life to the trade-union movement. His politics, interestingly, vividly illustrates his attitude towards the conflict between secular moralities, ideologies and political powers on the one hand – and the Word of God on the other.

A vociferous anti-Nazi, Barth was expelled by Hitler from his chair in Bonn, and forced in 1935 to return to his native Switzerland. By contrast, he never showed any particular hostility to communist forms of totalitarianism, and even refused – despite hundreds of indignant protests – to condemn such acts as the Russian invasion of Hungary of 1956. He did, however, sharply scold Western cold-war ideologists who advocated that Christianity be championed as a spiritual alternative to communism.

That Barth's political positions would arouse disagreement is easy to understand; that they cause bewilderment is puzzling, for Barth's politics are closely connected with his theological position.

Barth never would have *sympathised* with Hitler, but one rather doubts that Barth would have gained any notoriety as an anti-Nazi had Hitler not attempted to interfere with the doctrine of the Protestant churches in Germany. Indeed, had Hitler left the churches to go their own ways, at least doctrinally – had he not imposed his New Order on the Old Religion – it is not inconceivable that Barth would have behaved in a way which would have permitted him even to retain his chair. But toying with the intellectual tradition of de Lagarde, Langbehn and Moeller van den Bruck, Hitler attempted for a time to use the churches as vehicles of a 'German–Christian' Nazi ideology. It was principally *this*

Nazi policy that Barth opposed, and for essentially the *same* reasons that he opposed Protestant liberalism in 1918 and the idea of the 'Christian West' after World War II. According to Barth, it is contrary to the basic commitment of the theologian to the Word of God to allow *any* cultural ideology or morality, *good or bad*, to be incorporated into, or blended with, Christian doctrine. *Autonomous*, Christianity stands alone, in judgement on culture. The communists, unlike the Nazis, did not attempt to commit this particular sin: frankly atheistic, they were ready to destroy the churches if opportune but were rarely disposed to create a 'Marxist Christianity'. Barth anticipated that through skilful diplomacy and tact the churches could achieve a viable 'live and let live' accommodation with the communists. In this he may well have been politically naïve, but he was utterly consistent – even if one may sense a kind of madness about that very consistent order of priorities.

VIII

However rational and consistent Barth may have been, it remains true that he was at heart an irrationalist: he *was* committed dogmatically to the assumption that revelation occurred, that the Word of God had been given to man through Jesus, that the Bible was a testimony and report of this Word of God. Yet, as mentioned above, even here Barth was no more of an irrationalist – even if his irrationality was of a different sort – than are many well-known contemporary rationalists. I mentioned Ayer and Popper above, and will support my statement briefly here, not to defend Barth or to criticise Ayer or Popper, but to indicate the continuing importance of the problem of rationality.

I mentioned above, when discussing Kierkegaard, that way of thinking, sometimes called fideism, sometimes scepticism, that maintains that everyone must – for logical reasons – make an irrational commitment to his basic principles. To attempt to justify or to apologise for them leads, it is said, to logical paradox. Presumably Barth dropped Kierkegaard in the mid 1920s at least in part because of the enthusiasm with which his fideistic arguments for commitment and the absurd were taken up by thinkers whose attitudes to Christianity sharply opposed those of Barth. Fideistic arguments for irrational commitment had had historically, and have continued to have during this century, something like a boomerang effect. By providing an excuse for irrational commitment, the argument that rationality is ultimately limited may indeed enable a Protestant to make an absurd commitment without losing intellectual integrity. But if it does so then it does the same for any other commitments whatsoever.

Moreover, anyone who makes use of this excuse may not, with integrity, criticise the holder of a different commitment – a commitment not to Christ but to the Fatherland right or wrong, to the class struggle, or to just about anything else. One gains the right to be irrational oneself at the expense of losing the right to criticise anyone else for acting absurdly. One gains immunity from criticism for one's own commitment by making any criticism of alternative commitments trivially easy. One quickly reaches what R. H. Popkin, in a study of Kierkegaard, aptly described as an 'anarchy of private individual faiths that cannot be discussed or communicated'. This aspect of Kierkegaard's thought would ironically even give aid and comfort to the neo-liberal subjective ethical Christianity of Braithwaite!

To deal with such difficulties, various thinkers of a stripe quite different from that of Kierkegaard have taken various routes. Popper, for one, proposed to adopt a 'minimum concession to irrationalism'. Characterising himself as a 'critical rationalist', Popper wrote that 'whoever adopts the rationalist attitude does so because he has adopted, without reasoning, some proposal or decision, or belief, or habit, or behavior, which therefore in its turn must be called irrational. Whatever it may be, we can describe it as an irrational *faith in reason* . . . the fundamental rationalist attitude is based upon an irrational decision, or upon faith in reason. Accordingly, our choice is open. We are free to choose some form of irrationalism, even some radical or comprehensive form. But we are also free to choose a critical form of rationalism, one which frankly admits its limitations, and its basis in an irrational decision (and to that extent, a certain priority of irrationalism).'[5]

In *The Problem of Knowledge* (1965), Ayer also argues himself into an irrational commitment. There he calmly asserts that our standards of rationality need no rational justification because any such standard 'could be irrational only if there were a standard of rationality which it failed to meet; whereas in fact it goes to set the standard: arguments are judged to be rational or irrational by reference to it'. This is a monumental begging of the question, a logical howler which only someone with the acumen of an Ayer could make so elegantly and nonchalantly. Of course, *if* some particular standards and procedures of rationality, such as Ayer's, *are* the correct ones, then there can exist no other rational standards which are also correct but which can nevertheless invalidate the former as irrational. This 'if', however, marks a great assumption: *for this is precisely what is at issue* – and something that Barth would have challenged. Structurally speaking, Ayer's position is identical with that of Barth. Barth argued that apologetic defence or assessment of theology was to be outlawed *since* the Word of God *is* itself the standard or criterion which any such assessment would have to use – surely an assumption that Ayer would challenge. Both Ayer and Barth abandon *apologetics*, the sort of procedure which in theology tries to justify commitment rationally, and replace it with *kerygmatics*, which is devoted to the exposition and description of the fundamental message. Unable to justify his basic position, the logical empiricist, like the neo-orthodox theologian, begins to describe it. While Barth begs the question of the existence and righteousness of God and his Word, Ayer begs the question of the legitimacy of scientific induction.

Whoever then wishes to condemn Karl Barth for his stubborn Christian dogmatism in an 'era of scientific enlightenment' ought first to ask whether he himself can escape the quandaries of irrationalism and dogmatism into which even ardent rationalists like Popper and Ayer have been led. I believe that there is an escape,[6] but that it lies in a reconsideration of our entire theory of rationality, a theory that is sadly neglected by theologian and philosopher alike, and which is indeed probably the most basic source of conflict between morality and religion – or, for that matter, between one morality and another.

4 The Inseparability of Morality and Religion

> How each one of us, once we saunter past
> The first redemptions of inconstant life,
>   Repeat, repeat, repeat
>   The same dead measure
>   And the same dead beat,
> Open identical doors on identical death
> And feel ashamed of everyone we meet.
>
> David Stacton[1]

I

The title of this study is 'Morality and Religion', and we have, to be sure, discussed in the preceding three chapters the questions most often discussed in treatises on this subject. But a lingering, perhaps one should say 'haunting', question remains: namely, have we really said very much about morality and religion? We have talked rather freely of 'morality' and of 'religion', but what we have really most frequently referred to are moral codes and religious codes. What is a code? If we consult the dictionary, we find that a code is a systematic collection of statutes, body of laws so arranged as to avoid inconsistency and overlapping, set of rules on any subject, prevalent morality of a society or class, and so on. There are obviously not only moral and religious codes, but codes of all sorts: grammatical codes, legal codes, building codes, highway codes, codes of etiquette, codes of table behaviour, codes for letter-writing. I suppose that most people would say that although there are differences of differing degrees of importance amongst all these codes, there are also family resemblances in Wittgenstein's sense. Many people would add to this that it would be easy to give a rough ordering in respect of importance to the various sorts of codes I have mentioned. Religious codes would be most important; moral codes would be next, followed by legal codes. Such things as codes for good letter-writing would come near the bottom of most lists, and the others mentioned would presumably come somewhere in the middle. So it might seem. But here, as often, appearances are deceptive.

To give some examples: I have met persons who would have been only irritated to learn that I had dipped into their supply of letter-paper whilst a house guest but who would have stricken my name from the guest list had my bread-and-butter note begun 'Dear Joe', and ended 'Yours faithfully'. It is not even clear that such cases are cases of morality. The offended host might comment: *'ought'* has nothing whatever to do with it; one just *does not* (unless, perhaps, one is a bishop or clergyman) sign a letter: 'Yours faithfully' unless one has begun it with 'Dear Sir'! But this too needs qualifying. If 'one' is an Englishman, one does not do such things. But if one is an American, one might conceivably write one's British host, beginning 'Dear Brittanic Lordship', and concluding 'Cordially yours', and get very high marks from one's host: Americans have, after all, been known to commit yet greater gaffes. Of course the degree of obligation attached to learning codes of various countries and classes one may be visiting will vary enormously depending on circumstances. An American who drove on the right-hand side of the road in Britain would during most of this century have been thought to be violating not only the legal but also the moral code.

Such examples could be spelt out at some length: we could talk about persons who would lie, murder, rape and steal with less hesitation than they would sip port from a claret glass. And so on. But what is the point of all this?

There is no single point to be made. What needs calling to attention is the plain fact that many different codes govern different kinds of behaviour in which we may engage; that we are all at the same time following and failing to follow a number of different codes: whilst pouring the claret into the claret glass with one hand, I may be pocketing the host's silver with the other. More important, the degree of the emotion or the extent of the sanction applied to the breaking of some rule may have nothing to do with its place on our tentative pecking order. An immoral act may be shrugged off; an illegal act may be applauded; and a mild social *faux pas* regarded as unforgivable – all by the same persons. What is gauche may be thought far worse than what is wicked.

Yet to what profit would we deliberate whether Miss Emily

Post's book of etiquette contains *moral* codes or whether the codes contained therein are of some other character? Or to what purpose would we go searching the Pentateuch to sort out the religious code from the moral code from the eating code from the code of table manners? Probably to no purpose whatever – which leads one to doubt that it is important in most circumstances to distinguish except in the roughest way amongst the various codes that govern our behaviour. In the Pentateuch – and for that matter in Emily Post – we have woven together, in a rather intricate way, broad patterns of behaviour, patterns in which it is hardly possible or important to sort out, say, the religious elements from the moral.

The various sortings out that have been undertaken by philosophers and theologians, and to which I have referred in the preceding chapters, gained their importance, such as it was, from quite partisan goals. For example, were it possible to show that morality was indefensible without the endorsement of a god, that would provide some apologetic support for various beleaguered religions – from Plato's time to our own. And thus our attention to the 'Euthyphro Argument'. Or could it have been shown, as the Protestant liberals attempted for a time to do, that the Christian ethic was the most reasonable moral code, Christianity could have gained great strength at a time when it was under attack. In such partisan contexts, distinctions between morality and religion, and between moral and religious codes, may be important.

If one takes a broader view, however, I am inclined to think that these distinctions not only lose in importance, but can also become perniciously misleading. For this reason I have chosen to write in this closing chapter of 'The Inseparability of Morality and Religion'. First, however, I wish to state bluntly my over-all opinion of the possibility of moral action, an opinion that will seem unclear and perhaps even shocking at first, but which I hope will become both clearer and more plausible as the discussion develops.

We have been discussing moral, religious and other codes. Now it is conceivable – though actual instances must be rare – that some person would succeed in following *all* the rules of all the codes of behaviour required of him or adopted by him – religious, moral, legal, letter-writing, dinner-eating, building-constructing, and so on. A person who never makes the mistake

51

of breaking *any* rule whatsoever is at least imaginable. Those who have followed the Is/Ought discussion in the first chapter must allow that it remains an open question whether such a person *is* acting morally. But I wish to go further. I am convinced that such a person may well be one who never has and who never will act morally. I hope that it is obvious that I am using the words 'act morally' here in a special sense, though not in as odd a sense as it might at first be thought.

Now if I think that our imaginary but nonetheless possible perfect rule-follower may fail ever to act morally, it will surprise no one if I say that I believe that for most people moral action is virtually impossible. And if it is indeed true that 'ought' implies 'can', I am thus committed to the disturbing conclusion that *for most people it is false that they ought to act morally*. At most I could say that they ought to *try* to act morally. Indeed, I *would* say this, and confess in this connexion a personal allegiance to the passage from Hesse which I took as a motto for this study: 'It is necessary to continually attempt the seemingly impossible.' But this is a record of personal moral conviction, not a conclusion of analytical philosophising. Moreover, it is a normative moral expression that would have to be examined on its merits, and one too that would be rejected by some whose names have appeared in this study – by Karl Barth for instance, who would have rejected it as a species of 'moral titanism'. Karl Barth clearly recognised that normative moral positions of the type which I have just avowed were of a religious as well as a moral character.

To suggest what my conviction might amount to, and to distinguish it from a part of our philosophical tradition which I feel compelled to reject, I must now consider – and will reject – a most venerable and respectable distinction that British and American moral philosophers have made between morality and religion.

II

In his autobiography, Mr Leonard Woolf very forcibly protests Lord Keynes's familiar account of the kind of influence G. E. Moore had exerted over those who were later to become members of the Bloomsbury Group. Writing in 1938 about his early beliefs as an undergraduate at Cambridge, Keynes maintained of himself and his companions: 'We accepted Moore's religion . . . and discarded his morals . . . meaning by 'religion' one's attitude towards oneself and the ultimate and by 'morals' one's attitude towards the outside world and the intermediate.'[2] In *Sowing*, the first volume of his memoirs, Woolf calls this a 'distorted picture', stressing that he himself, Moore and their companions at Cambridge were all quite concerned about practical politics and public morality.[3]

If one examines the lives and records of those extraordinary individuals who belonged to the Cambridge and Bloomsbury Group, one is inclined to think that Keynes did indeed paint a rather romantic picture of their early days in Cambridge, and that Woolf's recollections are nearer to the truth. One's suspicion that Keynes's recollections are somewhat distorted is reinforced by Mr Michael Holroyd's recent biography of Lytton Strachey.[4] But it is not with such historical questions that I wish to deal here.

Rather, I should like to call attention to a point on which Keynes and Woolf appear to be agreed. Both maintain a distinction between one's religion – which is said to concern one's own inner states and one's attitude towards the ultimate – and one's morals – which are said to be directed towards the outside world and what Keynes calls the 'intermediate', which, amongst other things, are those things which are less than ultimate. This distinction has a venerable heritage in British philosophy, and it is still very much alive today. Interestingly, John Stuart Mill used a distinction very much like this to define his differences with the philosophy of Jeremy Bentham. In effect, Mill accused Bentham of leaving out of his account of human nature those things which Keynes brackets as religious. Bentham's general conception of human nature and life, Mill wrote:

furnished him with an unusually slender stock of premises . . . [he wantonly dismissed as] 'vague generalities' the whole unanalysed experience of the human race . . . the faculty by which one mind . . . throws itself into the feelings [of a mind different from itself] was denied him by his deficiency of Imagination. Self-consciousness, that daemon of . . . men of genius . . . never was awakened in him . . . he had never been made alive to the unseen influences which were acting on himself . . . his recognition does not extend to the more complex forms of [sympathy] – the love of loving . . . or of objects of admiration and reverence. . . . Man is never recognized by him as a being capable . . . of desiring, for its own sake, the conformity of his own character to his standard of excellence, without hope of good or fear of evil from other source than his own inward consciousness. . . . The sense of honour and personal dignity . . . the love of beauty, the passion of the artist. . . . None of these powerful constituents of human nature [so Mill concludes] are thought worthy of a place among the Springs of Action.[5]

Although Mill did not use the words 'religion' and 'morals' to define this difference, any more than Moore himself did, it is clear that Mill was accusing his mentor of having concentrated his attention on those things which Keynes was later to dub the 'moral aspects' of Moore's philosophy at the expense of what Keynes called the 'religious aspects', at the expense of those things, such as the love of beauty, and the development of inward consciousness, of which Moore was to write so powerfully in the famous last chapter of *Principia Ethica*.

This distinction between religion and morals, or, crudely, between the 'inner' and the 'outer' was, then, present in the very different forms of utilitarianism championed by Bentham and by Stuart Mill; it appears in the reaction to utilitarianism represented by Moore and the Bloomsbury Group. And, as I have suggested, it remains very much alive today – for example in what has come to be called the philosophy of 'negative utilitarianism' propounded by Popper. In the course of developing a Popperian account of ethics, one of his disciples has written categorically as follows: 'Morality should be understood in an extraverted way as concerned with our behaviour towards others. I draw a sharp distinction between a man's morality and his personal religion and private ideals.'[6]

III

This distinction between a man's behaviour towards others and his personal religion and private ideals does not bear examination. I do not wish – as must be clear from the foregoing

54

chapters – to reduce morals to religion or religion to morals. But I would maintain that these two, as defined by Keynes, and also as they manifest themselves in most of the great religions of the world, are so intertwined that an attempt to carry through the distinction amounts to something like an attempt to analyse the unanalysable. More important, and more pertinent, it hinders understanding of the development of either personal or social morality, understanding of the soul's conquest of evil.

I may as well state several further prejudices. One is that a far larger part of our behaviour towards other persons than we are inclined to admit is a tangled web of guilt, fear, shame, projection, exploitation, ignorance, lack of inner consciousness and the other stuff of which evil and arbitrary behaviour is compounded. Man, being in any case by nature a confused animal, and alarmed by these virtually unmanageable forces and states of being, erects various maxims, morals and wise sayings – indeed, occasionally even codifying them – to help him cope with his social environment. By and large he treats these codes uncritically, dogmatically, as magic charms against the unknown and unpredictable in himself and in his fellows. Another prejudice is that we tend to ignore these facts, and the complexities of interpretation that accompany them, and to ignore them perhaps especially when constructing our moral and ethical theories.

Although there may indeed be very little one can do about the way people behave towards one another, occasionally a few people can with some small measure of success embark on an at least partial conquest of evil. There is no one route to this conquest: the route may be sought, as in the Christian traditions, in the quest for what is called salvation. It may be sought, as for example in the philosophical psychology of C. G. Jung, in the quest for individuation, whose goal is 'wholeness'. It may be located, as many philosophers would prefer, in the Socratic tradition of searching for self-knowledge. Whatever the route, almost all such endeavours when successful involve what can be called heightened self-awareness, including some awareness of the evil of which one is capable – a subject to which I shall return. These quests are by and large *inner*; there is nothing 'unenlightened' about calling them *religious*. And without such inner quests, any so-called morality that may crop up in our external, *outer* behaviour is usually either conventional, coincidental or accidental. For our interpretation of our external social situation is subject to distortion by our failures in achieving a heightened inner self-awareness. This does not imply that we ought to compose ourselves in meditation, withdrawn from the social world, until some such time as we feel able to cope with it in full self-awareness. For paradoxically, our inner awareness develops as we reflect on the way in which our psyches impinge on the outer world, indeed, as we learn to differentiate between the *I* and the *not-I*.

IV

It would no doubt be helpful to analyse the meanings of various of the words and concepts I have been employing. But even to begin on this important and useful project would be to write another, or at least a far longer, book. Fortunately, the line of thought which I am pursuing is not utterly idiosyncratic, and several contemporary writers have discussed with considerable analytic penetration the philosophical issues involved in such a course. I have in mind such work as the discussion between R. W. Hepburn and Iris Murdoch on 'Vision and Choice in Morality', and P. F. Strawson's essay on 'Social Morality and Individual Ideal'. To these I refer my readers.[7]

For my own immediate purposes it will suffice to treat these themes in terms of some examples. I shall therefore draw on some stories from the case-books of modern psychology. They concern some adventures of a small boy whom we may call Christopher. Both stories were recalled by Christopher himself after he had become an adult, and were recounted in roughly the following form.

The first episode occurs when Christopher was eight years old, early in the first morning following the end of his Christmas holiday. We find him lying slumbering in bed, sleeping late, as he had done on many of the mornings during the holiday. Suddenly he is abruptly and painfully awakened: his mother seizes his hair, yanks him out of bed, and spanks him. She had been calling him repeatedly to rise, to wash and dress, and prepare for school But he had not heard; he had slept on; he was still on holiday. But not for long. Less than an hour later, on the way to school, trudging through the snow with his little sister, Mary, five years old, whom Christopher had to guide to and from school each day, he begins to cross-examine her about their mother. 'What do you feel about Mommy?' Christopher asks repeatedly. 'Don't you really hate her?' Sister protests her love of her mother; but Christopher is stubborn and persuasive – and he promises not to tell. Eventually, as they near school, Mary submits, and agrees that she really does hate their mother. That evening, after returning home from school, Christopher takes aside his mother to tell her: 'Mommy, Mary told me today that she hates you.' And then mother spanks Mary.

The second episode takes place about eighteen months later, in the summer, when Christopher was nine years old. His mother being devoutly religious, Christopher is sent regularly to church and taught religion at home as well. But he is a precocious lad and has already begun to doubt the stories of God and Jesus. We find him sitting on the porch of his family's house, in the warm summer evening, talking with his father. 'Daddy,' he asks, 'was there really a Jesus? Did all those miracles really happen?' His father replies: 'Well, we don't really know; they may have – but perhaps not.' Christopher turns away almost immediately, goes inside to his mother, and reports accusingly: 'Mommy, Daddy says there wasn't any Jesus.' There followed an extraordinarily heated quarrel between Christopher's parents, one which his father, as was usual, lost.

We could hardly even begin to explore here the nuances latent in the report of these two episodes. But it is obvious what pattern is present in both these stories about a shockingly clever wicked little good boy who had not the slightest idea what he was doing, and yet at the same time in a sense may have known very well what he was doing.

In the first episode Christopher had felt himself wrongly punished – and quite possibly he was: mother perhaps ought to have been particularly indulgent at the end of the school holiday. But we do not know how things were with her: perhaps she had been having a deserved holiday too. Christopher, at any rate, was furious. His fury expressed itself most crudely, as hate for his mother – and perhaps for all things feminine: his sister, the school, his teachers, his having to care for his sister on the way to school. But Christopher also loved his mother; and he knew from his teaching and from his religious and moral training that one ought only to love one's mother. He could not openly express his hostility towards his mother, and yet he could not bear *not* to have it expressed. So he virtually forced his little sister – only five years old and hardly aware of what had happened – to express, to *voice*, the evil sentiment. And then Christopher promptly saw to it that the crime was punished: he tattled on his sister, and saw her suffer the same punishment, spanking, that he had earlier endured.

The behavioural pattern is the same in the second episode. Christopher was unable or unwilling to express his forbidden doubts about religious teachings; he probably suspected that his father also harboured such doubts, for we are informed that his father did not go to church very often; and so, in a 'man to man' talk, he tricked his father into voicing the forbidden doubts. And once again Christopher saw to it that the crime was punished: his father was spanked verbally by his mother and stalked off in despair to the neighbourhood pub – perhaps thereby corroborating his wickedness in his son's eyes. In this extraordinary way Christopher's religious doubts were laid quietly, but oh so devilishly, to sleep, not to be yanked awake again for nearly a decade, at which time he was thrust into a severe neurosis.

If one is horrified by Christopher's behaviour, at the same time one need not hide a certain admiration for the skilful way in which he was able to manipulate his social environment. One of the chief reasons for this, of course, was its predictability, in particular the predictability of his mother. When we take a closer look at his mother's predictability, we find that it consists largely in her rigidity, her unconsciousness, her lack of development – failures that were doubtless partly due to and partly reinforced by the dogmatic moral maxims which she virtually used as magic charms to deal with her own social environment. Christopher appears to have been able to predict, almost to the details, the sorts of actions she would take in response to the information which he fed her. She did not question his reports; she did not inquire how these issues – Mary's suddenly voiced hate for her or her husband's religious scepticism – had been raised. When her code appeared to have

58

been violated she did not pause to make inquiries; she sought revenge. The life of his family appears to have revolved around Christopher in a curious way. Christopher, one might think, was a kind of vampire who cast a spell on the members of his family, sucking their lifeblood to nourish his existence. Christopher used the members of his family, one after the other, to commit the crimes he himself would like to have committed, and then called on his mother to bring down God's wrath on the criminals. But he could do this only because he knew that his mother would not *look* at the situation, but would *blindly* defend her moral magic. How the archetypes must have howled: for morality by magic is self-defeating, sustaining unconsciousness; putting nascent awareness to rest; spreading, not dispelling, man's confusion.

V

Did Christopher do wrong? One may smile at the question; and yet, what expression is one supposed to wear on one's face when one discovers that there are two so-called 'schools of thought' about such questions which predominate in our ethics textbooks: one of them counselling us to examine motives; the other, consequences? Whatever the school-philosophers might say, I am inclined to doubt that we can give a very enlightening answer to our question by looking at Christopher's motives or intentions on the one hand, or by looking at the consequences of his behaviour on the other. Take the question of consequences first. One could of course say that any behaviour that led to Mary's being unjustly spanked was wrong. But to dismiss the issue so easily is rather flippant. Apart from the fact that it took the mother, as well as Christopher, to bring off the unjust spanking, one might well wonder whether that spanking might not have been one of the best things that ever happened to Mary? Perhaps it jarred her into erecting some defences against the 'loving brother' who may have guided her safely to school each day, but who did not hesitate monstrously to misuse her when it suited his purposes. We do not know.

We do know that Christopher himself later suffered from a serious neurosis. But to say that even this was necessarily an unfortunate consequence of his behaviour is to have made a host of assumptions. Hardly any psychiatrist, at least on the basis of the meagre evidence adduced here, would admit that Christopher's neurosis – even if we accept that that neurosis was unequivocally bad *for him* – was the direct effect of either or both of these two episodes. It may have been, or it may not; clearly there are many children who have gone through experiences prima facie more damaging than these, and emerged relatively unscathed. Similar remarks might be made about any causal connexion that might be traced between these actions of Christopher's and later unhappy relationships between Christopher's father and mother, or his mother and sister. It is evident that Christopher was already working within a highly charged and neurotic situation which was by no means his own creation.

One's perspective on this situation is not made much clearer by abandoning an attempt to evaluate in terms of consequences, an *Erfolgungsethik* or negative utilitarianism, and looking instead, in the manner of the traditional *Gesinnungsethiker*, to Christopher's 'motives' or 'intentions'. It is no news to those interested in philosophy that the notions of motivation and intention are filled with obscurity; but even if one overlooks this fact, one may raise the question whether, whatever they may mean, a satisfactory account of them must not presuppose a degree of self-awareness which we have no reason to suppose that Christopher possessed. In fact one might, if one did not look too closely, defend both Christopher's motives and his results in the second episode. In the moral universe then inhabited by Christopher, to doubt religious teaching was wrong, and to see that such doubts were punished was right. So his motivation – and the immediate result he achieved – could both be excused; some perhaps would even praise them. But of course to say this is not to look very deep.

So let us try to probe somewhat deeper. We have implied that a satisfactory account of motivation or intention – whether good or bad – must presuppose a degree of self-awareness which Christopher did not have. Christopher was of course a child. Is this what is after all meant by saying that children are innocent? One would not gather so from the literature about the 'lack of innocence' of children which has been produced during the past half-century. For in this, what has usually been stressed is their lack of innocence in a very primitive sense of the word: we have learned that children also inhabit the world of *sex*, that they are very aware sexually, and to that extent are not the innocent babes that some people once fancied them.

But perhaps our concept of innocence contains much richer connotations; and we mean, or people meant, when we or they speak or spoke of the innocence of children, that they *behave*, they do not *act*; that they literally do not know what they are doing. But to argue in this direction is to risk letting off everyone as innocent – or rendering us all children. After all, did Christopher's mother, who was no child, know what she was doing? How much self-awareness did she enjoy? How much self-awareness do most people enjoy? 'Father, forgive them, for they know not what they do', we read in the Gospels. I have already indicated my own rather pessimistic attitude towards such questions. Heinrich Zimmer was, I daresay, right when he wrote: 'Guilt and innocence are rarely obvious. They are unapparent, interwoven intimately with each other in a marvellously convoluted design.'[8]

Another example will help to make this clearer, an example which I draw from an essay by Professor Donald MacKinnon.[9] Discussing various misuses to which the Christian doctrine of redemption through sacrifice may be put, MacKinnon writes:

> To sacrifice ourselves is, it is said, to realize the image of the crucified, whereas the self-sacrificing may simply be mutilating himself, purposively destroying the sweetness of existence in the name of illusion, in order to make himself a hero in his own eyes. . . . Those who are familiar with the problems of the care of old people will know very well what I call the phenomenon of the 'human sacrifice', the daughter in a large family who is described as 'devoted to her parents' (the language has a ritual quality), and who is therefore chosen to look after them in their decline. Not infrequently she is the victim of various sorts of spiritual blackmail. Her patience perhaps is exhausted by her mother's near senile cantankerousness and she is told 'you will be sorry one day, dear, when I am dead and gone'; (and a discreet sob accompanies the last words). She sees her life slipping from her and still she is held in the vice-like grip, I will not say of dedication, but of convention consecrated by the ecclesiastical image of

sacrifice. The ethic of sacrifice indeed provides a symbolism under which all sorts of cruelties may be perpetrated, not so much upon the weak as upon those who have been deceived by a false image of goodness.

Just as, in the former examples, we asked whether Christopher did wrong, we might in this instance ask whether the self-sacrificing daughter was doing right. Here again we have a particular example of innocence, guilt, exploitation, projection, all working together to the destruction or at least impoverishment of several human beings. 'Girls withering into ladies,' G. B. Shaw's heroine remarks: 'ladies withering into old maids. Nursing old women. Running errands for old men. Good for nothing at last. Oh, you can't imagine the fiendish selfishness of the old people and the maudlin sacrifice of the young.'

VI

I have indicated, by these examples drawn from intimate personal relationships, my prejudice that neither an ethic of motive nor an ethic of consequence is much help in judging such relationships and the behaviour that occurs within them. In doing so I do not wish to suggest that the various sorts of motivational and utilitarian accounts of moral judgement are useless – let alone to suggest that they have been authored with malicious intent! Both are necessary; neither is sufficient; nor are they sufficient when taken together.

Were I to attempt to gather together some of my own intuitions about these matters, I should have to say something like the following. We can neither *act morally* nor evaluate with much competence the actions of other persons without an extraordinarily deep knowledge of ourselves and of our surroundings. Without such deep understanding we discriminate only in the clumsiest way between good and bad consequence or between good and bad intention. An important reason for this is that we are much at the mercy of our projections – that is, in the psychological sense, those interior states which we impose on the external world in the course of interpreting it.

In speaking of projection I do not wish to labour the obvious or familiar, but if an example is needed one would be of the shy man who, because of his own fears and hostilities and aggressive feelings towards other persons, projects these feelings onto certain of those other persons – even where the real attitudes of those persons do not merit any such projection – and assumes, or better, acts as if, these other persons harboured aggressive and hostile feelings towards him. When such psychological phenomena become systematised, as they do in occasional individuals, such conditions as paranoia may develop. But one need not adduce such unattractive states to elucidate the notion of projection: 'falling in love' is one of those rather more pleasant states of affairs where our projections may take possession of us.

Consider again the problem of evaluating in terms of consequences, in the light of what has just been said. It would seem clear that a utilitarian ethic is wrong if only because our actions have unintended consequences that cannot possibly be predicted in advance. But even if this were not so, it is not likely that much consensus could be achieved about which consequences were unsatisfactory. Shaw wrote in the preface to *Major Barbara*: 'It is exceedingly difficult to make people realise that an evil is an evil.'[10] And indeed, some of the most topical moral questions today stem from disagreement about what is evil: about whether some purported consequence of a particular moral or legal code is really unsatisfactory. Take the public debates in Europe and America about capital punishment, about contraception, about the optimum size of families, about homosexuality, about prostitution, about the use of drugs. On the more controversial questions our feelings about desirable and undesirable consequences, conditioned as they are by projection, do not lead to agreement.

Which brings us back to the distinction advanced above by such as Keynes between our personal ideals and our social behaviour. Paradoxically, it might well turn out that a kind of utopianism in personal morality or religion might be a necessary condition for a satisfactory anti-utopianism in social life – so intertwined are these two arenas of human behaviour. One might, for instance, recall psychological and sociological discussions of the high cost in anxiety and other ills persons pay personally for the sublimation required individually to build a civilised society, achieve some measure of rationality, and act in terms of social decency and warmth. And still, in full awareness of this prospect of suffering, some may still prefer such an ideal.

Morality indeed cannot be restricted to our social behaviour. For some psychological self-consciousness on the part of an individual – which *may* be achieved only through his following of some such personal ideal – is required if he is to have proper sympathy for other persons, if he is to avoid such things as projections in evaluating social situations and in not feeling feelings of moral revulsion where such feelings are not due. In the event of conflict between a man's 'morality' and his 'private ideals' (or religion) should either one or the other always prevail? A certain stick-to-it-ivity regarding his private ideals may at least sometimes be required if a man is to evaluate particular social situations with the maximum of objectivity.

If our interpretation of our social environment and its ills then may be, and indeed usually is, severely distorted by our internal states, how does one achieve an internal psychological state, a relationship between consciousness and the unconscious, which does not precipitate a distorted view of the social environment? The question just raised is hardly one I can answer to anyone's satisfaction, including my own. There are as many routes charted to this state of being as there are psychologists, not to mention religious leaders. Nonetheless, one can make a few remarks that are relevant. For one thing, as I have already indicated in speaking of Keynes and Moore, these internal quests might just as well be called religious. For another thing, they are not exactly pleasant: they may involve great stress and deep suffering. Even Freud, one of the apostles of such self-awareness as may be achieved through psychoanalysis, occasionally wondered whether the whole process – and civilisation into the bargain – was worth the effort. One of the unpleasant things that are required if such quests are to be even moderately successful is a deep appreciation of the evil of which one is capable – whether this is expressed as one's 'sinfulness', as it might be within the Christian tr adition, or as a recognition of one's knavery, to speak in terms that could be given an entirely pagan interpretation.

There is nothing novel about what has just been said. The late C. G. Jung, for example, wrote as follows of the conquest of evil:[11]

The individual who wishes to have an answer to the problem of evil, as it is posed today, has need, first and foremost, of self-knowledge, that is, the utmost possible knowledge of his own wholeness. He must know relentlessly how much good he can do, and what crimes he is capable of, and must beware of regarding the one as real and the other as illusion. Both are elements within his nature, and both are bound to come to light in him, should he wish – as he ought – to live without self-deception or self-delusion.

We have such advice not only from psychologists like Jung, but also from our mythology and folklore. In Heinrich Zimmer's collection of stories, *The King and the Corpse*, which I mentioned earlier, one reads of legendary figures like Conn-eda, an Irish prince, or, again, of the Hindu king after whom the collection is named: two heroes who are distinguished – and also imperilled – by their guilelessness and innocence, their trustfulness, their lack of imagination for evil, which, paradoxically, put them at the mercy of the forces of evil. These figures, like many hero figures of legend and myth, must transform their inner selves by going through perilous trials in which they are initiated into evil – an initiation process which requires them to doff, or sacrifice, their earlier personalities, to acquire a penetrating knowledge of the dark as well as the light side of things, a more penetrating knowledge of both inner and outer 'social life' as it really is, to die to their old selves and to be 'born anew', and thereby to become fitter to perform their kingly tasks: 'to dispense justice as well as mercy'.[12] Only then do they become capable of moral *action*.

The figures just mentioned are princely, heroic, strong, which helps to confirm that the conquest of evil and the attainment of the ability to act morally is rarely achieved by those who are weak psychologically and intellectually. The weak may well do things that are good; they rarely do good things. Nietzsche wrote in *Zarathustra*:[13] 'There is nobody from whom I want beauty as much as from you who are powerful: let your kindness be your final self-conquest. Of all evil I deem you capable: therefore I want the good from you. Verily, I often have laughed at the weaklings who thought themselves good because they had no claws.'

65

That Cambridge and Bloomsbury Group whose memories I invoked at the beginning of this chapter were preoccupied with the development of the interior life at the same time that they were able to deal shrewdly with the outer world. And in the course of their interior quests they did not preen themselves only on the pretty. Was it not, after all, the Hogarth Press that pioneered the translation and discussion of Freud in England? Those associated with the group were also strong, whatever their physical and psychological ailments may have been. Russell, Moore, Keynes, Leonard and Virginia Woolf, Morgan Forster: these persons transformed not only themselves and one another; in our century they transformed logic and epistemology, ethics, economics, publishing – and a part of the tradition of the English novel into the bargain. They were capable of enormous evil, and – knowing it – did considerable good. As those who supped with them, or were reviewed by them, knew well, they had claws. Yet perhaps the self-conquest that at least a few of them attained – and which some weaker men mistook for weakness – lay in the kindness and gentleness of which they were capable, that which one finds perhaps best expressed in the novels of Forster. Although these individuals were, then, engaged in a conquest of evil, although they even were, one might say, searching for salvation, it is well to remember that they were hardly Christians: they often referred to themselves as pagans. Indeed, it is not really very interesting to remark that the epigraph of *Howards End*, 'Only connect', expresses a profoundly un-Christian sentiment.

Notes

Chapter 1

1. Theodore Parker, 'The Transient and the Permanent in Christianity', in Perry Miller (ed.), *The Transcendentalists* (Harvard University Press, Cambridge, Mass., 1950) pp. 259–283.
2. Plato, *Euthyphro*, xii 10.
3. P. T. Geach, 'The Moral Law and the Law of God', chapter 9 of *God and the Soul* (Routledge & Kegan Paul, London, 1969).
4. One of the most insistent on this point has been Karl Popper.
5. See 'JAMA' ccv 9 (26 Aug 1968) 28.
6. Ibid.
8. W. W. Bartley, III, 'Theories of Demarcation between Science and Metaphysics', in *Problems in the Philosophy of Science*, ed. I. Lakatos and A. E. Musgrave (North-Holland Publishing Co., Amsterdam, 1968) pp. 40–119, esp. p. 48.

Chapter 2

1. Quentin Bell, *Bloomsbury* (Basic Books, New York, 1968) p. 28.
2. W. W. Bartley, III, *The Retreat to Commitment* (Knopf, New York, 1962; Chatto & Windus, London, 1964). See also the extensively revised German translation, *Flucht ins Engagement* (Szczesny Verlag, Munich, 1964).
3. R. B. Braithwaite, 'An Empiricist's View of the Nature of Religious Belief', in I. T. Ramsey (ed.), *Christian Ethics and Contemporary Philosophy* (S.C.M. Press, London, 1966), or in John Hick (ed.), *The Existence of God* (Macmillan, New York, 1964). The study was first printed separately by the Cam-

bridge University Press as the Eddington Memorial Lecture for 1955.

4. The neologism is Braithwaite's idiosyncratic way of rendering the Greek ἀγάπη into English as an adjective.

5. Braithwaite, in *Christian Ethics and Contemporary Philosophy*, p. 68.

6. These discussions, together with Braithwaite's reply, are reprinted ibid.

7. John Macquarrie, *Twentieth-Century Religious Thought* (S.C.M. Press, London, 1963) p. 312.

8. Ibid., p. 316.

9. Renford Bambrough, *Reason, Truth and God* (Methuen & Co., London, 1969) p. 74.

10. Ved Mehta, *The New Theologian* (Harper & Row, New York, 1965) p. 70.

11. Albert Schweitzer, *The Quest of the Historical Jesus*.

12. See my discussions of Barth in *The Retreat to Commitment*, but more especially in my 'Rationality versus the Theory of Rationality', in M. Bunge (ed.), *The Critical Approach to Science and Philosophy* (Free Press, New York, 1964).

13. *The I Ching, or Book of Changes*, the Richard Wilhelm translation rendered into English by Cary F. Baynes (Princeton University Press, 1968).

14. Heinrich Zimmer, *The King and the Corpse* (Meridian Books, New York, 1960).

15. David Stacton, *Kaliyuga* (Faber & Faber, London, 1965).

16. Karl Bühler, *Sprachtheorie: Die Darstellungsfunktion der Sprache* (Gustav Fischer Verlag, Stuttgart, 1965).

17. This was added by Bühler's student, K. R. Popper. See Popper, *Conjectures and Refutations* (Routledge & Kegan Paul, London, 1962) pp. 134 and 295. See also, on the relations between Popper and Bühler, the following: W. W. Bartley, III, 'Sprach- und Wissenschaftstheorie als Werkzeuge einer Schulreform: Wittgenstein und Popper als österreichische Schullehrer', in *Conceptus* (Munich and Innsbruck, April 1969); W. W. Bartley, III, 'Theory of Language and Philosophy of Science as Instruments of Educational Reform: Wittgenstein and Popper as Austrian Schoolteachers', forthcoming in *Boston Studies in the Philosophy of Science*, ed. R. Cohen and Marx Wartofsky; and W. W. Bartley, III, 'Die österreichische Schulreform als die Wiege der modernen Philosophie', in

68

Club Voltaire: Jahrbuch für Kritische Aufklärung, vol. iv (Rowohlt Verlag, Hamburg, 1970).

18. Bühler, *Sprachtheorie*, p. 28.

Chapter 3

1. Karl Barth, *The Epistle to the Romans*, translation from the sixth edition, including author's preface to the English edition and prefaces to the first through sixth editions (Oxford University Press, 1968).

2. Around 1927 Barth abruptly dropped Kierkegaard: in his enormous twelve-volume *Church Dogmatics* Barth mentions Kierkegaard about twenty times, often in small type and in passing, and usually to criticise one or other of his minor ideas. In a brief autobiography which appeared in 1945, Barth does not even list Kierkegaard amongst those thinkers who shaped his doctrinal standpoint; and in *Die Protestantische Theologie im 19. Jahrhundert* (1947), published in abridged form in English as *Protestant Thought from Rousseau to Ritschl*, Barth mentions Kierkegaard only three times. See my essay, 'Everybody's Kierkegaard', in the *New York Review of Books*, 28 April, 1966, pp. 11–15.

3. Karl Barth, *Evangelical Theology* (Holt, Rinehart & Winston, New York, 1963) p. 131.

4. Karl Barth: 'Wolfgang Amadeus Mozart', in *Religion and Culture*, ed. Walter Leibrecht (S.C.M. Press, London, 1959) pp. 72–3.

5. K. R. Popper, *The Open Society and Its Enemies*, chapter 24, first through third editions. For a similar statement by Popper, see his paper 'Utopia and Violence', *Hibbert Journal* (1948). In the fourth edition of *The Open Society* Popper began to modify his position somewhat, but I do not believe that his attempts to rectify his system have as yet been successful.

6. See my book *The Retreat to Commitment*, and also my paper 'Rationality versus the Theory of Rationality', in *The Critical Approach to Science and Philosophy*.

1. Quoted by Frederic Spiegelberg, *Living Religions of the World* (Prentice-Hall, Englewood Cliffs, N.J., 1956) p. 129. Stacton's poem is taken from an unpublished manuscript, 'The Death of Bosola'.

2. John Maynard Keynes, 'My Early Beliefs', in *Two Memoirs* (New York, 1949) p. 82.

3. Leonard Woolf, *Sowing: An Autobiography of the Years 1880–1904* (Hogarth Press, London, 1960) pp. 146 ff.

4. Michael Holroyd, *Lytton Strachey*, vols i and ii (Heinemann, London, 1967–8).

5. John Stuart Mill, 'Bentham', in, for example, John Stuart Mill, *On Bentham and Coleridge*, intro. F. R. Leavis (New York, 1962), or in John Stuart Mill, *Utilitarianism*, ed. Mary Warnock (London, 1962).

6. J. W. N. Watkins, 'Negative Utilitarianism', in *Proceedings of the Aristotelian Society*, suppl. vol. (1963) 96 ff.

7. These essays are reprinted in *Christian Ethics and Contemporary Philosophy*.

8. Zimmer, *The King and the Corpse*, p. 224.

9. D. M. MacKinnon, 'Moral Objections', in *Objections to Christian Belief* (London, 1963), esp. pp. 23 ff.

10. G. B. Shaw, *Major Barbara* (Dodd, Mead, New York, 1941).

11. C. G. Jung, *Memories, Dreams, Reflections* (Pantheon, New York, 1961) p. 330.

12. Zimmer, *The King and the Corpse*, p. 42.

13. Friedrich Nietzsche, *Thus Spake Zarathustra*, in the chapter 'On Those Who Are Sublime'. See also Walter Kaufmann's discussion in *The Owl and the Nightingale* (Faber & Faber, London, 1959). Parts of sections II through VI of the present chapter are drawn from my essay 'The Soul's Conquest of Evil, in *Talk of God*, ed. G. N. A. Vesey (Macmillan, London, 1969).

Bibliography

Chapter 1

Plato, *Euthyphro*.

Kurt Baier, *The Moral Point of View* (Cornell University Press, Ithaca, N.Y., 1958).

W. W. Bartley, III, 'Theories of Demarcation between Science and Metaphysics', in I. Lakatos and A. E. Musgrave (eds), *Problems in the Philosophy of Science* (North-Holland Publishing Co., Amsterdam, 1968).

Philippa Foot (ed.), *Theories of Ethics* (Oxford University Press, 1967).

W. D. Hudson (ed.), *The Is–Ought Question* (Macmillan, London, 1969).

G. E. Moore, *Principia Ethica* (Cambridge University Press, 1954).

Chapter 2

Renford Bambrough, *Reason, Truth and God* (Methuen, London, 1969).

W. W. Bartley, III, 'Rationality versus the Theory of Rationality', in M. Bunge (ed.), *The Critical Approach to Science and Philosophy* (Free Press, New York, 1964).

W. W. Bartley, III, *The Retreat to Commitment* (Knopf, New York, 1962; Chatto & Windus, London, 1964).

R. B. Braithwaite, *An Empiricist's View of the Nature of Religious Belief*, The Eddington Memorial Lecture (Cambridge University Press, 1955).

Karl Bühler, *Ausdruckstheorie: Das System an der Geschichte aufgezeigt*, second, unaltered edition, with a foreword by Albert Wellek (Gustav Fischer Verlag, Stuttgart, 1968).

Karl Bühler, *Sprachtheorie: Die Darstellungsfunktion der Sprache*,

second, unaltered edition, with a foreword by Friedrich
Kainz (Gustav Fischer Verlag, Stuttgart, 1965).

John Hick, *Evil and the God of Love* (Macmillan, London, 1966).

Albert Schweitzer, *The Quest of the Historical Jesus* (Black,
London, 1910).

David Stacton, *Kaliyuga* (Faber & Faber, London, 1965).

David Stacton, *Segaki* (Faber & Faber, London, 1958).

Chapter 3

Sir Alfred Ayer, *The Problem of Knowledge* (Penguin, London,
1956).

Karl Barth, his writings; in particular, those referred to in the
text of this study.

W. W. Bartley, III, 'Everybody's Kierkegaard', in *New York
Review of Books*, 28 April, 1966, pp. 11–15.

W. W. Bartley, III, 'Karl Barth: "The Last of the Protestants" ',
in *Encounter* (March 1970).

Søren Kierkegaard: his writings, of which there are many
editions. Consult Robert Bretall (ed.), *A Kierkegaard
Anthology* (Princeton University Press, 1951).

Sir Karl Popper, *The Open Society and Its Enemies* (Routledge &
Kegan Paul, London, first through third editions).

Chapter 4

C. G. Jung, *Answer to Job* (Meridian Books, New York, 1960).

D. M. MacKinnon, *A Study in Ethical Theory* (Collier Books,
New York, 1962).

Erich Neumann, *The Origins and History of Consciousness*, vols i
and ii (Harper Torchbook, New York, 1962).

I. T. Ramsey (ed.), *Christian Ethics and Contemporary Philosophy*
(S.C.M. Press, London, 1966).